KU-406-137

MESSY MATHS

A Playful, Outdoor Approach for Early Years

JULIET ROBERTSON

independent
thinking press

First published by

Independent Thinking Press
Crown Buildings, Bancyfelin, Carmarthen, Wales, SA33 5ND, UK

www.independentthinkingpress.com

Independent Thinking Press is an imprint of Crown House Publishing Ltd.

© Juliet Robertson 2017

The right of Juliet Robertson to be identified as the author of this work has been asserted by her in accordance with the Copyright, Designs and Patents Act 1988.

Photography © Jane Hewitt 2017, except pages 5, 13, 20, 24, 31, 33, 34 (measuring stick and cut sticks), 35, 40, 43, 47, 49 (top), 52, 57, 72, 78, 104, 106, 109, 112, 117, 129, 135, 142, 143, 145, 153, 154, 157, 168, 172, 173, 177, 180, 182 (bottom), 184, 187, 192, 195, 197, 210, 211, 215, 216, 218, 219, 224, 227 © Juliet Robertson 2017, page 11 © Julie Lyon 2017.

Jane Hewitt has asserted her right under the Copyright, Designs and Patents Act 1988, to be identified as illustrator of this work.

First published 2017. Reprinted 2017 (twice), 2018 (twice), 2019.

All rights reserved. Except as permitted under current legislation no part of this work may be photocopied, stored in a retrieval system, published, performed in public, adapted, broadcast, transmitted, recorded or reproduced in any form or by any means, without the prior permission of the copyright owners. Enquiries should be addressed to Independent Thinking Press.

Independent Thinking Press has no responsibility for the persistence or accuracy of URLs for external or third-party websites referred to in this publication, and does not guarantee that any content on such websites is, or will remain, accurate or appropriate.

British Library Cataloguing-in-Publication Data.

A catalogue entry for this book is available from the British Library.

Print ISBN 978-1-78135-266-3
Mobi ISBN 978-1-78135-292-2
ePub ISBN 978-1-78135-293-9
ePDF ISBN 978-1-78135-294-6

Printed and bound in the UK by
Gomer Press, Llandysul, Ceredigion

Praise for *Messy Maths*

Wow, what a fabulous book! Incredibly comprehensive and full of exciting possibilities, it should convince anyone of the huge potential of the outdoors.

Messy Maths will motivate the reader to harness the outdoors' special nature for embedded, meaningful mathematical thinking and satisfying, deep-level learning – I particularly love the mathematical garden. Why would you stay indoors?

Jan White, mudologist and consultant for outdoor provision in the early years

Even if only a fraction of the ideas contained in this book are put into practice, they will still make a huge difference to children's knowledge and understanding of maths. What really struck me whilst reading this book was a recognition of the problems we create for ourselves with older children because we don't spend enough time developing their conceptual understanding – leading to situations in which 10- and 11-year-olds have no real concept of what a metre actually looks like, or what a kilogramme feels like. Through her practical, easy-to-apply and – in most cases – zero-cost strategies, Juliet Robertson offers the perfect solution.

Rooted in exceptional early years practice, *Messy Maths* is an indispensable guide to getting maths right – not just with our youngest learners, but with all children.

Jonathan Lear, teacher, speaker and author of *Guerrilla Teaching*

Messy Maths is a wonderful resource! Aesthetically beautiful with its engaging photographs, it is easy and inspiring to read and offers meaningful and practical ideas for exploring maths outside of the classroom.

The most valuable aspect from my point of view is the encouragement to find maths in the everyday outdoors. It is in the recognition of these teachable moments that we, as early years educators, can bring maths to life for young children.

Mairi Ferris, Director, Stramash Outdoor Nurseries

We learn with our hearts and our hands before our heads. That holds true for every aspect of the curriculum and indeed for life – but doubly, trebly so for learning the foundations of mathematics at an early age.

Except for a chosen few, I don't believe there is such a thing as a natural mathematician. As with language, music and science, our skills develop organically over time and are grounded in our childhood experiences. Children today have less time outdoors than ever before, with fewer opportunities to try out experiments and play with maths on their own. So it's more important than ever that schools take learning outdoors, allowing children to build their foundation of concepts and language naturally and confidently.

This is a great follow-up to *Dirty Teaching*. It stands alone in its own right, however, giving teachers, child-minders and all educators (including parents) the confidence to see the mathematics all around us and to help children draw out the concepts they are exploring in their play.

I highly recommend *Messy Maths* to teachers working at all stages and in all manner of early years settings. You'll come away inspired – ready to get outdoors and help the children you work with feel super confident in their mathematical language and practical application of mathematical reasoning. I bet you'll get better at estimating weights and lengths too!

Cath Prisk, Global Campaign Director, Outdoor Classroom Day

This book is dedicated to my sister, Sophie,
who loved maths.

Contents

Most of my class are very confident at climbing trees. One day I had a new little girl who was not so sure. She stood and watched the other children for several minutes before one of her friends shouted for her to come up the tree. 'Come on, Alex. It's good up here. It is so high and you can see really far to the other side.' Another child added, 'Alex, you look tiny down there. Climb up and you will be big again. Miss Dean will be really small if you climb up.'

Alex continued to watch the others, remarking, 'Miss Dean, it's too scary up high.' One child, Rylan, said, 'It's okay, I can come down and help.' Rylan climbed down from the tree and went over to Alex. After a little bit of encouragement, Alex began to cautiously climb the tree. Rylan directed her using a host of positional language: 'Put your foot a little higher' and 'Move to the side by the fat branch.'

I was able to expand and support this language throughout the experience, and each time Alex got a little higher you could see her confidence growing more and more. When she had got as high as she could, we talked about what she could see and compared this to being on the ground.

When her mum came to pick her up, Alex was excited to tell her what she had done that day. She described her experience using the positional and size related language she had been exposed to. It was a fabulous learning experience for Alex, Rylan and me.

Louise Dean, early years teacher,
Redgate Community Primary School, Formby, Liverpool

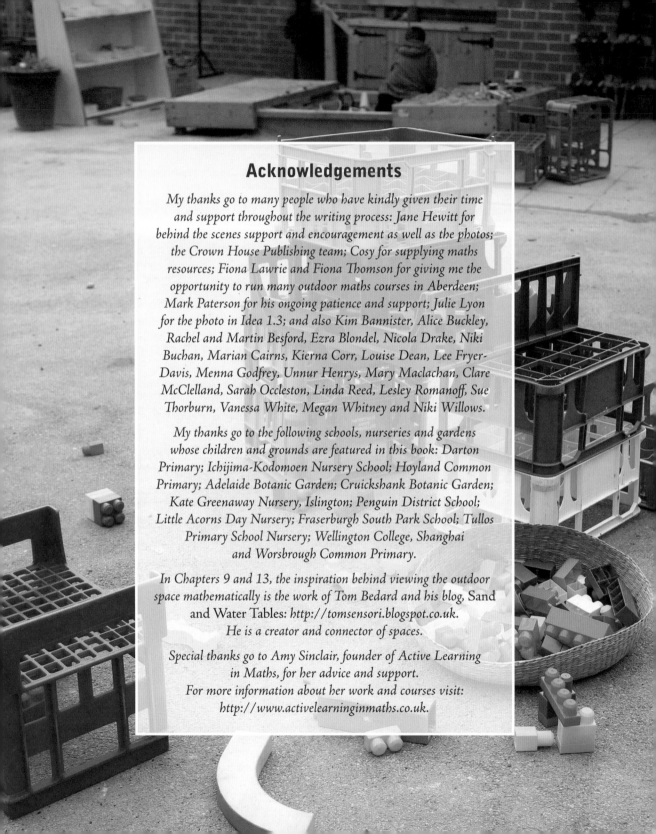

Acknowledgements

My thanks go to many people who have kindly given their time and support throughout the writing process: Jane Hewitt for behind the scenes support and encouragement as well as the photos; the Crown House Publishing team; Cosy for supplying maths resources; Fiona Lawrie and Fiona Thomson for giving me the opportunity to run many outdoor maths courses in Aberdeen; Mark Paterson for his ongoing patience and support; Julie Lyon for the photo in Idea 1.3; and also Kim Bannister, Alice Buckley, Rachel and Martin Besford, Ezra Blondel, Nicola Drake, Niki Buchan, Marian Cairns, Kierna Corr, Louise Dean, Lee Fryer-Davis, Menna Godfrey, Unnur Henrys, Mary Maclachan, Clare McClelland, Sarah Occleston, Linda Reed, Lesley Romanoff, Sue Thorburn, Vanessa White, Megan Whitney and Niki Willows.

My thanks go to the following schools, nurseries and gardens whose children and grounds are featured in this book: Darton Primary; Ichijima-Kodomoen Nursery School; Hoyland Common Primary; Adelaide Botanic Garden; Cruickshank Botanic Garden; Kate Greenaway Nursery, Islington; Penguin District School; Little Acorns Day Nursery; Fraserburgh South Park School; Tullos Primary School Nursery; Wellington College, Shanghai and Worsbrough Common Primary.

In Chapters 9 and 13, the inspiration behind viewing the outdoor space mathematically is the work of Tom Bedard and his blog, Sand and Water Tables: http://tomsensori.blogspot.co.uk. He is a creator and connector of spaces.

Special thanks go to Amy Sinclair, founder of Active Learning in Maths, for her advice and support. For more information about her work and courses visit: http://www.activelearninginmaths.co.uk.

Introduction

The world is a mathematical place. For young children who are naturally curious there are shapes, numbers, moving objects and patterns to behold, things to count and investigations to be undertaken. It is a creative, challenging and wondrous way of looking at life and exploring the world.

Maths is an inherent part of being human. Framing the world through maths helps us make sense of what is happening and how it affects us. It can provide order and certainty as well as help to explain random events. For little children, maths is not just a cognitive process. It is also a social, emotional and physical experience. A problem shared is a problem halved. Think back to your own experiences of maths at school and how you felt about learning it. Consider how children need lots of physical experiences that embody what maths is all about. The only way to understand the concept of weight, for example, is to repeatedly lift, move and carry a range of heavy and light objects.

Being outside enables connections to be made between the hands, heart and head, laying the foundations for more complex work as children grow, develop and learn. The natural and built worlds provide dynamic and constantly changing environments, offering an endless supply of patterns, textures, colours, quantities and other attributes that underpin much of the necessary early maths experiences.

This book has several aims:

■ To help educators consider their own understanding and confidence in developing mathematical provision, making the most of the outdoor space in their setting – whether this be a nursery, playgroup, child-minder's back garden or a nature kindergarten.

■ To enable children to have lots of informal, spontaneous mathematical experiences which are child initiated and child led. When children play, they are in control of their learning and it has meaning and purpose to them.

■ To provide a range of open-ended ideas for adapting to children's interests as part of a playful approach to learning maths concepts. This is about educators being responsive to the needs and interests of children.

■ To make the most of any outdoor space as a context for maths. We need to consider how time in greenspaces such as woodlands, parks and beaches contributes to children's mathematical experiences, as can the use of natural materials.

I believe that every child and adult is mathematically able. We all have different strengths and abilities within maths. By sharing ideas and enjoying mathematical conversations, we can deepen our understanding. For children who require additional support, we need to be sensitive to their

needs. Use language and communication methods appropriate to their abilities, have fun and focus on precisely what each child can do. They may surprise you and extend your learning just as much as you do theirs.

Being outside makes maths feel real rather than disconnected from our daily lives. And real maths is really messy! Aside from mud pies and puddles, the cognitive processes involved mean it is not a smooth linear pathway of learning but rather an interconnected network. Children need time to make sense of abstract mathematical ideas through experiential processes, along with opportunities to ponder, enjoy and discuss the concepts encountered. Lots of playing along the way is a must.

How to use this book

Messy Maths has been written for educators who work with children aged between approximately three and six years of age. It is not a 'how to' guide, rather a handy reference book: a source of ideas about tapping into the outdoors to help children become confident and skilled in thinking about, using and exploring mathematical concepts as they play outside. Many aspects of any early years maths curriculum can be addressed without the need for structured activities, but through developing the four R's of routines, resources, the responsibilities of adults and reimagining the environment. This means looking at our outdoor space with a mathematical lens and considering the possibilities. This is discussed in Chapter 13.

Suggestions for integrating maths into routines have been amalgamated in Chapter 12. The intention is to provide explicit examples of possibilities to help develop creative, progressive and flexible approaches to embedding maths.

Throughout the book I refer to 'gathering circles'. These are times when the children have gathered together and are ready for, and interested in, undertaking a shared event. Sometimes gathering circles happen naturally outside, such as when lunch is shared together in a wood. More often, they are informal occurrences when children playing together congregate to view an exciting discovery or to simply relax and chat to each other.

A positive approach to being outside

Throughout the book, there are lots of ideas and accompanying photos that contain elements of risk. In line with best practice, it is important that you consider all the suggestions on a case-by-case basis to determine whether they are appropriate for the developmental stage and learning needs of your children. The adults who work with your children need to have the competence and confidence to ensure the routines, resources and environment are as safe as is necessary. Remember to undertake risk–benefit assessments, in line with your establishment's health and safety policies and procedures, for anything you feel needs it, be this using tools and ropes, exploring the mathematics of fire, climbing trees and other experiences involving height, moving heavy objects, working off-site or near water, and so on. *Messy Maths* is about enabling outdoor practice but every educator and setting needs to undertake this within a framework of safety.

Likewise, it is important that wherever you are working you follow the land access laws of your country. Being respectful of others, leaving no trace of your presence and considering the impact of your practice on the environment are all part of our responsibilities as educators.

The basics

The core building blocks of maths matter as much outside as they do indoors. Derek Haylock and Anne Cockburn propose that a 'mathematical concept can be thought of as a network of connections between symbols, language, concrete experiences and pictures'.[1] This means children need to:

■ Recognise the symbols used in maths.

■ Know and understand the language used.

---

1 D. Haylock and A. Cockburn, *Understanding Mathematics for Young Children: A Guide for Teachers of Children 3–8* (4th edn) (London: SAGE Publications, 2013), p. 27.

■ Be able to create a mental or actual image of the concept.

■ Have concrete experiences and relevant contexts for working in maths.

Most difficulties arise when not all of these elements are experienced or if they are not connected in a meaningful way. Undertaking maths activities outside provides an ideal environment for these connections to happen. It allows for skills and concepts learnt in one context to be readily applied to another.

Ann Montague-Smith and Alison Price replace concrete experiences with more specific detail.[2] They suggest that two important elements of maths are 'physical materials' and 'real world scripts'. They state that real world tasks matter but also cite the value of 'script' in songs, rhymes and stories. These scripts provide children with relevant language and enable them to act out and retell stories that use the language in context. Daniela O'Neill, Michelle Pearce and Jennifer Pick studied the relationship between children's narrative abilities in pre-school and found a predictive relationship with their later mathematical ability.[3] For me, this is about enabling emotions to be expressed and time being made for children to make sense of concepts through role play, creative work and imaginative play. It is about employing strategies which engage children.

The other work which has influenced my thinking has been that of Czech mathematician Milan Hejný. His approach to maths teaching and child development uses twelve principles.[4] These are grounded in common sense. The first principle is 'building schemata'. Hejný suggests that children need to construct a network of mental mathematical schemata based upon their real life experiences – that is, to understand something you need to be able to connect the concept or idea to previous experiences. The Hejný approach uses experiences familiar to young children (such as walking) as a starting point to develop maths concepts and mental patterns and images.

The use of sticks is another example of a schema advocated by Hejný. Many children are familiar with and use sticks in their play, so the use of a stick to explain and illustrate mathematical thinking is building upon a known item. It is easy to make the link between a stick on the ground and a line drawn on a piece of paper. Thus the connection between using symbols and two-dimensional images is facilitated.

Finally, the concept of embodied cognition is particularly relevant in the context of how children grow and develop their mathematical understanding. This is about the acquisition of maths concepts being grounded in body movements and through interactions with the environment. Think about how children use their fingers as they learn to count. Hortensia Soto-Johnson suggests that highlighting students' gestures, repeating their words, mimicking their gestures and asking

---

2 A. Montague-Smith and A. Price, *Mathematics in Early Years Education* (3rd edn) (Abingdon: Routledge, 2012), p. 16.

3 D. K. O'Neill, M. J. Pearce and J. L. Pick, Predictive relations between aspects of preschool children's narratives and performance on the Peabody Individualized Achievement Test – Revised: evidence of a relation between early narrative and later mathematical ability. *First Language*, 24 (2004): 149–183.

4 See: http://www.h-mat.cz/en/principles.

probing questions can all help them to articulate their thinking.[5] By paying attention to gesture, educators can learn more about children's mathematical reasoning and misconceptions.

One metre challenge

This activity is useful to undertake with parents or colleagues. In an outdoor space, ask everyone to create a line that is exactly one metre long using natural materials they can find.

Afterwards, discuss how each person worked out their metre. Provide measuring tapes or metre sticks so the results can be checked. Whilst there is always variation, most people rely on their previous knowledge about the approximate length of a metre. Some people relate it to a part of their body, others use a known reference such as the number of times an A4 sheet of paper fits into a metre. This 'knowing' is what children need to acquire through lots of practical play-based explorations of maths.

---

5 H. Soto-Johnson, Learning mathematics through embodied activities. *American Mathematical Society* (8 February 2016). Available at: http://blogs.ams.org/matheducation/2016/02/08/learning-mathematics-through-embodied-activities/#sthash.LeIk8Lne.dpbs.

Outside, ensuring children have plenty of access to natural environments where they can develop physically through movement and interactions with nature is particularly beneficial. The inextricable link between the development of the brain and body is summed up nicely by Jan White: 'Movement and action give children intuitive, bodily-felt meanings about concepts that will later be understood more intellectually (such as many of the ideas we use in maths like weight and size). Embodied experiences also create deeper, more lasting memories which can be drawn on in different ways.'[6] In other words, children need to use their whole bodies to learn maths.

The educator's role

The role of adults is flagged up repeatedly in books and research articles. Pradnya Patet provides an eloquent summary of how educators can empower young mathematical minds.[7] She argues that mathematical proficiency does not appear on its own but needs careful scaffolding that is meaningful and relevant. When children play you can see their level of understanding in a genuine context.

As educators we can facilitate maths play outdoors in many ways:

- We can set up outdoor areas in mathematical ways and embed maths into our routines.

- When redesigning an outdoor space, we can take account of features that can facilitate mathematical dialogue, explorations and investigations (see Chapter 13).

- We must make the most of teachable moments to introduce the language and specific skills that enhance children's ability to reason mathematically. We should also offer suggestions, statements and challenges which encourage children to articulate their thinking. We want children to ask questions, discuss problems that arise and to not fear making mistakes. Errors are crucial to learning.

- We can be ready to build upon what children are doing through their play, their interests and what they like doing outside. The possible lines of development can be a mix of resources, investigations and simple prompts that support independent mathematical play.

- We can ensure that children themselves are the overwhelming evidence of their own learning and achievements in maths, rather than focusing on a paper-dependent system.

---

6 J. White, *Every Child A Mover: A Practical Guide to Providing Children with the Physical Opportunities They Need* (London: Early Education, 2015), p. 16.

7 P. Patet, Empowering mathematical minds through play. *Community Playthings* (8 September 2015). Available at: http://www.communityplaythings.co.uk/learning-library/articles/empowering-mathematical-minds.

Modelling a mathematical mindset

How adults respond to children regarding maths really counts. Jo Boaler's book, *Mathematical Mindsets*, advocates practical strategies for ensuring that the adults who work with children adopt a growth mindset approach that makes maths enjoyable and achievable.[8]

Everyone can achieve in maths, and we are always improving our knowledge and understanding. I believe a key benefit of outdoor play is that we can build confidence in maths concepts before children even perceive their play as mathematical, and in doing so we help to lessen, challenge or even prevent the development of negative connotations about the subject.

Practitioners need to actively show an interest in, and enthusiasm for, maths. Modelling maths activities, showing children how to use different resources, using mathematical language and being up for having fun with maths makes a big difference. Pass on a love of numbers.

---

8 J. Boaler, *Mathematical Mindsets: Unleashing Students' Potential Through Creative Math, Inspiring Messages and Innovative Teaching* (San Francisco, CA: Jossey-Bass, 2016).

CHAPTER 1

Where's the Maths In That?

The purpose of this chapter is to provide some starting points for reflecting upon the mathematics which is inherent in children's play. We work in an educational culture in which the pressure is on us to be continually interacting, extending children's learning through dialogue, modelling what is expected or leading a structured activity. The best thing we can do is stop, step back, observe what the children are doing and reflect upon the maths we are witnessing.

By unpicking what we see children doing from a mathematical perspective, it is easier to consider the resources, experiences and conversations that are required to develop the skills, knowledge and understanding they need to gain next. This chapter includes several exercises to help you do this and considers some of the issues facing educators when providing maths opportunities outside.

Idea 1.1 Ensuring national expectations are achieved

In many countries there are statements about what children need to know and be able to do in order to reach a desired standard at a given age. Educators are required to make assessments and use their professional judgement to ensure that every child achieves what is expected of them. A range of evidence is needed. Within early years settings, most of this evidence can be collated through observations of and discussions with children. Also, there are lots of games and fun ways of eliciting a child's level of attainment.

Children need a balanced education that takes account of their social, emotional, physical and cognitive development. There is a lot of evidence which all points towards outdoor free play in a natural setting as providing the optimal conditions for this to happen, when combined with sensitive, nurturing adult support.[1] Being outside means children can apply their knowledge and skills across a range of real life contexts, thereby consolidating their understanding.

To isolate elements of maths without considering this wider context is not giving either the child or the subject an opportunity to flourish. Curriculum guidelines always advocate an embedded approach. It is up to those of us who work with children to interpret this advice in a holistic way that matches best practice and research. A standardised maths test is only one small part of the bigger picture. It will not be able to ascertain a child's ability to use maths for real. A couple of years after I began teaching, I met a five-year-old pupil on her own in a local shop. She told me with delight that she would have 72 pence change from one pound after she had bought her Mars

---

1 The Children & Nature Network features a comprehensive collection of research which is curated and updated at: http://www.childrenandnature.org/learn/research/.

bar. As a young teacher, I realised that my focus on national standards had limited my own expectations about what this child could do.

Try to avoid getting hung up on evidencing what you have planned and provided. Taking photos of and writing lengthy documentation about what you have covered in a day or week is no indication of what the children have learnt. Shift the focus from what you are doing as a teacher to what your children know and demonstrate in their daily lives at home and in school.

Idea 1.2 Looking through a mathematical lens

Anything we do can be described from a mathematical perspective. It can enrich and help us to understand our world a little better. Imagine a child climbing a tree. There may be little to suggest that they are doing anything mathematical in this act. Yet if we stop and think, there is quite a bit of maths involved:

■ Constant estimation: will this branch be strong enough to support my weight? Can I reach the next branch?

- Informal measurement: is the branch too thick for me to hold? How much longer before I reach the top?

- Ongoing problem-solving, critical thinking and reasoning: which branch is the best to use now? What ones are best avoided? Will I be able to get down from here?

- Position and movement: will my body fit between the branches? Can I climb through and up?

Take opportunities to observe children playing outside and look at what they are doing through a mathematical lens. Write down your observations and share them with colleagues. It is important that you articulate your thoughts so that you can practise using mathematical language and are precise when doing so.

Idea 1.3 Unpicking the maths

To help you unpick the maths, you need to get to grips with the specific maths you observe. In the photo a child has laid out a line of objects – it is an example of pattern making.

To break down observations, ask yourself questions such as:

- What do you mean when you say 'pattern making'?

- Tell me more about this idea …

- What is the maths involved in this aspect of pattern making?

- What would motivate this child to extend their pattern making?

Once you step beyond the generalisation of pattern making in your thinking, then a range of possible lines of development emerge. You can see that the pattern is a repeating sequence of three objects. Furthermore, the sticks are in descending order of size. Now it is easier to consider ways of extending the learning, such as:

- Extending the pattern – could the child add in a fourth object to the sequence?

- Changing the pattern to make it different but equally interesting.

- Recreating the pattern yourself but changing an attribute or aspect to see if the child or other children can work out what you have done.

Idea 1.4 There's maths everywhere

Keep a maths diary for a day when working with the children. Every time you see a mathematical moment, jot it down. For example, if you have free flow between indoor and outdoor spaces, this is number bonds in action: if there are thirty children in your class and twelve are outside, then eighteen must be inside. Then one child goes to the toilet and suddenly the number bond becomes compounded into $17 + 1 + 12 = 30$. From here, you can begin to see the maths in everything!

Idea 1.5 Developing your mathematical vocabulary and knowledge

As educators we need to be able to understand and apply mathematical terms. For instance, if you don't know what the difference between cardinal, ordinal and nominal numbers is, then take the time to find out. An online search of children's maths websites or video clips is a friendly starting point; some of the explanations on adult websites can get unnecessarily complicated.

Talk with your team to develop a shared understanding and agree definitions – take, for example, the difference between weight and mass. In their everyday lives, people tend to use the term *weight* when actually they mean the *mass* of an object. Thus, you will need to decide how to approach this sort of situation. Mathematical definitions take significantly more effort to embed, so staff, children and their families will need to know and understand the significance of each word.

Develop pocket-sized prompt cards or put up notices in key places to remind all the adults in your team. This means the children receive consistent messages and maths becomes woven into more of their everyday conversations. The use of word clouds can be a useful visual approach.

anticlockwise
nearly
minute
yesterday
later
evening
afternoon midnight
almost
month
clockwise second
noon **fast**
quickly next **week** **midday**
pendulum clock **time** **digital** **slow**
year **now** century **season**
forever
never day soon
date morning sunrise **night**
hour tomorrow analogue
sunset

Idea 1.6 The mathematical value of loose parts

It takes time and practice to be able to see and articulate the mathematical value in commonly found materials and repurposed items. It is often dependent upon how a child decides to use an object. A useful exercise is to illustrate the maths potential of an ordinary item such as a bread crate. It works well as a group exercise: focus on creating challenges and problems to solve that you know the children may choose to undertake with friendly support and interest from an adult.

Bread Crates

Can you find any numbers on this crate? Why are they there?

How many crates do you need to make a den? Does it matter which way up they stand?

What can fit inside a crate? Is there anything you can find which is a perfect fit?

What is the tallest stack you can make with the bread crates? How will you measure its height? Is it taller than you and how do you know?

Is it possible to make a platform so you can travel from one side of the playground to the other without touching the ground? What is the smallest number of crates you can safely use?

What objects can be posted through a crate, or several crates stacked up?

Does the shape of an object affect the speed at which it can fall through the holes? What about the position of an object before you drop it?

Can you invent a game which involves posting objects, numbers or money through the bread crate?

What patterns can you see in the bread crate? Try painting over and around them to find out.

Idea 1.7 Parents and my line manager expect there to be proper maths resources outside

Clarify what your manager or the parents mean by this sort of comment. It is quite possible that they have not had time to consider maths in an outdoor context before, and therefore are looking for the reassurance of a number line hung on a fence or a range of shapes with key words stuck on a shed. In this situation, suggest that those who are concerned spend some time with you outside, where you jointly consider what is working well and what could be even better. Remember to:

■ Ensure that your maths resources are clearly labelled and accessible.

■ Draw the visitors' attention to children's mathematical play and explain how you build upon this (see the table in Idea 1.11).

■ Play one or two of your children's favourite maths games outside – there are lots of examples in this book. Draw the observing adults' attention to the mathematical learning taking place.

Idea 1.8 Learning from what children are doing, not what you want them to do

It is easy to set up an outdoor space with a preconceived agenda, only for this to be ignored by the children, who have different ideas. This does not mean that the learning is lost but that the emphasis is likely to have changed. When I visited one nursery, pots of water and paintbrushes had been set out beside a wall as a mark-making activity. A child came up to the area, discarded the paintbrushes and started throwing water at the wall. Afterwards, he rushed up to me and asked me to come and have a look at the splashes. From our discussion, I could determine that the child knew the difference between words such as 'big', 'small', 'little' and 'large'.

As a result of this interaction, I realised that having a few maths resources in my pocket would be very useful. Since then, I carry a thin one metre rope so that when the children talk about size I can model the measuring process. See Idea 2.14 for other useful pocket-sized resources.

Idea 1.9 Making maths personal and meaningful

Children want maths to be personal to them. For instance, they take pride in recognising a pattern they have created which may match a design on an item of clothing they are wearing.

Sit down and reflect upon your interactions with the children during the course of one day. Think about ways in which you could, another time, make explicit links to maths concepts by directly relating the maths to the child and their interests. Very often, there are enthusiasms which can be built upon and developed year on year. For example, dinosaurs seem to stand the test of time, so begin to record and capture any dinosaur action so that you can develop maths through passion-based play!

Dinosaurs

What is the actual height of your favourite dinosaur?

Find something outside that is the same height. How can you be sure it is?

How many pine cones laid end to end would show this height on the ground? How does this compare to your height?

How much space would your dinosaur need to make a nest and go to sleep? How many sleeping dinosaurs would fit in your outdoor space?

Find out the mass of a dinosaur egg. How many stones must you collect to represent how heavy the egg would feel?

Is the egg heavier or lighter than a car? How can you find out?

Estimate the size of a dinosaur footprint. Make a life-sized cardboard cut-out and discover what the dinosaur could step on if it ran through your outdoor space.

How many steps would it take to cross the outdoor space? Do you think this would be different for another dinosaur? How do you know?

Create a small model dinosaur island for your dinosaurs. How would you separate the carnivores from the herbivores?

Idea 1.10 Contextualising the learning

In each of the forthcoming chapters there are a selection of open-ended ideas for adapting to a range of contexts. I feel that it is important to focus primarily on the maths concepts that need to be developed and on how this can happen outside. However, one of our key roles as educators is to ensure that these ideas are presented in ways which match the children's interests.

Over time, you will develop a deep knowledge of what can be done to extend children's learning based upon their passion for being superheroes or their fascination with worms.

> There are many benefits to ensuring that maths is contextualised, particularly outside where the real world can bring the subject to life. For space related maths, the children created the universe in the playground using found objects and made patterns of stars. We stayed in role, put on our astronaut suits and went hunting for patterns in 'space' (outside).
>
> After visiting a garden centre, a group of children drew and measured plants. They weighed soil from the outside planters and created chalk flowerbeds featuring plants of specific sizes on the paving slabs. At one point the paving slabs became the shelves of a garden centre where they drew objects for sale using patterns.
>
> When I introduced contextualised maths, it became a favourite part of the day – for me as well as the children.
>
> Linda Reed, head teacher, Garnetbank Primary School, Glasgow

Idea 1.11 When children won't play with maths resources

It is easy to assume that putting maths resources outside will make the children want to play with them. This is a top-down approach which I have found to be largely unsuccessful. Start by observing the children playing outside. What do they enjoy doing?

On wet, cold days, investigating puddles is popular with the children. When observing children playing in a puddle, a number of themes tend to emerge. I use these to consider mathematical activities outside.

What are children doing?	We can extend this play by …
Stepping into puddles to see how deep they are	■ Modelling the use of a measuring stick to see how deep a puddle is ■ Drawing a number scale on the back of our boots to measure the depth and showing this to the children ■ Wondering aloud if this puddle is the deepest in the vicinity
Filling containers, pouring and emptying	■ Offering different sizes of container ■ Offering different shapes of container ■ See Chapter 6 for volume and capacity ideas
Jumping up and down, making a splash	Challenging the children to: ■ Splash all the water out of the puddle – this is volume displacement in action ■ Find out which object makes the biggest splash when dropped into the puddle. Does the mass or shape of the object affect the size of the splash? Does the height from which it is dropped make a difference? How can we record or measure the size of the splash? ■ Jump over the puddle – this is exploring the concept of length in a physical way

Take time to build up a range of challenges, games, questions and experiences linked to the maths resources. Children will be creative and inventive with open-ended resources, but if you have spent time exploring, playing and reflecting upon the resources, you will be able to facilitate the next steps more easily because you know the range of possibilities.

Idea 1.12 The joy of repeated play

Within your class, it is very likely that you have a group of children who, when given the opportunity to play freely, will default to a preferred activity or behaviour – for instance, a desire to run around or always choosing to play on bikes.

Rather than trying to work against the tide of interest, spend time integrating the maths into the children's favourite play. Very often the children are up for it and interested if you are too.

On the following pages, ideas for each of these interests have been pulled together to illustrate the possibilities.

How fast can we run?

Challenge children to time themselves running a particular distance or circuit.

Model and show children how to do this by:

■ Estimating the length of time it will take before checking the actual time

■ Singing a song

■ Counting numbers

■ Using a sand-timer

■ Using a digital device

■ Using an analogue clock and following the hand that shows the seconds

■ Using an analogue stopwatch

■ Using a count-down timer

Does running up or down a hill affect the speed at which we run? How can we find out?

Races

What races can we invent?

■ Obstacle courses

■ Bean bag on the head

■ Potato and spoon

■ Bunny hops

Who came first, second and so on? How can we record this?

How many children can run at once? How can we make this happen without bumping into each other?

Where can we race to? On a walk this may be a feature such as a gate where we stop and wait.

How many laps can we run?

Can someone check and record the number of laps?

What if we cycled or pushed a trolley instead of running? How does this change the speed and distance that we travel?

Creating running tracks

What do we need to make a track?

How long is our track and how do we know?

Can we draw a map of our track so we can remember what it looks like?

Collecting games

What is the fastest time in which we can pick up objects, and can we sort them correctly when we put them elsewhere?

Can we run to different stations and do a physical activity? For example:

- Ten star jumps
- Run round a tree three times
- Touch the ground then jump up five times

How far can you run, and how do you know?

Estimate and check using a range of standard and non-standard tools. For example:

- Trundle wheel
- Long tape measure
- Piece of rope marked with metres
- Timing ourselves as we run using different timers

Wonder aloud how to find out how far it is to a key feature and how long it may take to get there. Encourage estimates.

Position and movement

Suggest to the children that they place equipment to move up and over, through, under, etc.

The children can photograph each other and add simple labels to a story or sequencing book about their activity.

Encourage the children to make simple games that involve running around or moving through the equipment.

How many steps does it take us when we run to different places outside?

How can we record where we ran to and in what order?

Is it quicker to run as a relay team?

Would carrying something make us faster or slower? How can we find out?

In how many different ways can we get from A to B? Can we walk, run, move sideways, etc.?

Recall what happened using ordinal language: first, second, third, etc.

Playing with wheeled toys is a natural extension of running around. The table below shows possible lines of development that extend the running around section.

Developing a sense of space and shape

Do we have enough space to park the bike?

Can we park accurately between the lines?

What happens if we park in the wrong place? What will be the fine for removing the wheel clamp or getting the bike back from the bike pound?

Challenge children to create rear-view mirrors – a practical introduction to symmetry.

Position and movement

Can we reverse park?

Which bike is best for:

■ Manoeuvring around the outdoor space?

- Building up speed?
- Carrying a heavy load?

Exploring pattern

Which bike has the best tread pattern? Can the children recognise the different bikes by their tyre pattern?

Number matters

What numbers would you put on your number plate and why? Can you read the numbers?

Number the bikes. Has the correct bike been parked in the correct bay?

Are locks needed to park the bikes safely? How do we use a combination lock?

Do we need a licence to ride the bike? What is the date of issue, licence number and expiry date?

Create a bike hire shop

Hire your favourite bike:

- Find the correct change to pay for the duration of the hire time.
- Note the hire time.
- Book your turn by signing your name on a chart depicting the choice of bikes available and their attributes: colour, type, number of wheels, etc.

Offer free one litre bike washes

If more than this volume of water is used, then the children must pay for the extra litres.

Use a ten litre jerry can to share out the correct amount of water into one litre tubs.

Attach a one litre milk bottle with a small hole at the bottom to a bike. The child must fill up at a garage once it is empty – just like petrol. Don't forget to put the cap back on!

Weight and mass

Provide trailers for carrying different loads. Which objects are the heaviest and require more effort to transport?

Natural environments also lend themselves to repeated explorations.

Poking mud with a stick

How deep is the mud and how can we work this out?

Is there is enough mud to collect in a tub?

I wonder if you can …

- Find a stick long enough to poke in the mud?
- Find anything that is light enough to stay on top of the mud?
- Find anything heavy enough to sink into the mud?
- Make a hole that won't be refilled with mud?
- Smear mud in a very thin layer on the ground?
- Lift up a large dollop of mud with your stick?

How many little sticks can be pushed into the mud with your big stick?

How far away from other children do we need to be when playing with mud? How can we measure this distance?

Does the time of year or season affect the properties of mud?

When is the mud dry? When is it most wet and runny?

How far can we safely flick mud and how can we measure this? Footprints? Sticks laid end to end? Or something else?

What patterns can we make in the mud with a stick? How long do they last before they disappear?

What type of stick works best for poking mud? Is it …

- A long or short one?
- A wide or narrow one?
- A heavy or light one?

How high can you lift your stick before smacking it into the mud? Does the height at which you lift your stick affect the sound made, or is it how hard you hit the mud?

How hard do you have to hit the mud before splats occur? How many splats can you make?

CHAPTER 2

General Advice

This chapter covers suggestions that are relevant to all areas of maths and are useful to apply throughout your provision.

Idea 2.1 Puppets, toys and fantasy characters

The use of different characters to help children learn about number concepts is a widely applied technique and is relevant to outdoor play. Often, children will more readily respond to a puppet asking a question or be more willing to explain to a teddy bear who doesn't understand how to count. A small finger puppet can be kept in your pocket for this purpose. Alternatively, impromptu characters can be quickly made from sticks, cones and other natural resources.

A series of little stories can be developed around a maths character. My favourite is Sammy the rope snake who helps the children learn about fractions, conservation of length and the concept of one metre.[1] Once the children realise Sammy's abilities, they also want to make up stories about Sammy and show him mathematically interesting things.

Idea 2.2 Playing maths games outdoors

Maths games can be easily adapted to match a child's interests and give the children an opportunity to develop and practise key skills. The use of materials such as counters, dice and layouts provide a concrete context. They can be used to introduce the skill of recording symbols and information relevant to the outcome of the game. The language of maths is introduced informally through the conversations that happen.

Children should be invited, rather than expected, to play organised games. It's a way of learning which doesn't suit everyone. Also, some games may lack relevance to a child or they may need to watch other children play before being willing to join in.

A powerful approach is supporting children to invent their own games as part of their free play. These may be based upon known games but often they are more directly linked to role play or physical play and can be spontaneous. Rather than disturb a good game, observe what is happening,

---

1 J. Robertson, Introducing Sammy the 1-metre rope snake, *Creative Star Learning* (12 January 2016). Available at: http://creativestarlearning.co.uk/early-years-outdoors/the-magic-of-1-metre-rope/.

perhaps take a photo or video, and afterwards invite the children involved to share their experiences. The adult can scribe or record the sequence, rules, consequences and questions if the children wish for a record to be kept.

These games may be physically active and involve running about a lot or be about repeated patterns of behaviour in a role play context. The rules created (and broken) enable the children to understand cause and effect, the consequences of particular actions and overall outcomes. The learning that happens is a useful foundation for many aspects of maths in the years to come.

The invention of games, or the playing of traditional games, is a platform for conversations about chance and probability through questions such as:

■ Is the game fair?

■ Does everyone have the same chance of winning?

■ What has to happen so that you have a good chance of winning?

■ What might happen to make you think you have bad luck in this game?

Strategy and logic games are discussed in Chapter 8. These are a good starting point as they are quick and simple to make and learn.

Idea 2.3 Developing a repertoire of mathematical songs, rhymes and stories for using outside

Songs, rhymes and stories are a valuable way to introduce or reinforce key aspects of maths, such as counting in the right order. Music is part of every culture and almost all children love singing and dancing.

Compile a list that works well outdoors where there is more space for actions and moving about. The songs and rhymes can link directly to features in the environment – for example, you can sit on a real log to sing 'Five Little Speckled Frogs'. Songs such as 'One Man Went to Mow' are fun to act out and help the children to learn the concept of counting on or adding one more. These can all be adapted to fit your children's interests.

It can also be fun to make up simple number rhymes in context. For instance, one group of children I worked with developed the following tree climbing rhyme. The children climbed up into the tree when they were called by the previous child to do so.

> One little child sat up in a tree
> She looked out saying, 'Climb up here with me.'
> Two little children sat up in a tree
> They looked out saying, 'Climb up here with me.'

If you have a group singing a number song or rhyme, once the children know the song well enough, ask them to draw their own representations of the song. This will provide an insight into their understanding of the maths behind a song or rhyme.

When children are ready to access formal approaches, you could begin to model a mathematical representation of the number work as the children sing. With the song 'Ten Green Bottles', the mathematical representation may look like this:

$$10 - 1 = 9$$
$$9 - 1 = 8$$
$$8 - 1 = 7$$
and so on

Maths songs and rhymes can also be used for:

- Transition work, such as putting on outdoor clothing.
- Walking from one place to another. The beat or rhythm can help to reinforce aspects of number pattern and relationships. Marching tunes and group songs used to be popular in days gone by to help pass the time. Songlines are used by the Aboriginal people of Australia to explain how to get from one place to another using key features of the landscape.
- Developing safety routines such as gathering and head counts (see Idea 12.11).

You need to know the mathematical purpose of each song, rhyme and story and spend time ensuring that this is illustrated in fun and interesting ways for the children. Ask for their thoughts and ideas here. Some examples include:

- 'One Elephant Went Out to Play' – adding one to a set.
- '1, 2, 3, 4, 5, Once I Caught a Fish Alive' – counting.
- 'Five Little Speckled Frogs' – number bond of five, subtracting one from a set of objects, adding one to a set of objects.
- 'One Man Went to Mow' – memorising a sequence, adding one object to a set.
- 'Ten Green Bottles' – subtracting one object from a set, number bond of ten.

Idea 2.4 Family fun with maths

Parents and carers can make a vital difference to a child and their understanding of, and interest in, maths. Rather than overwhelm parents with suggestions, it can work well to drip-feed mathematical opportunities into the ongoing activities in your setting.

- Throughout the year, have a changing display or a series of blog posts which highlight maths play in different contexts based upon your off-site visits. For example:
  - Playing in a local park
  - Regular sessions at a local woodland
  - On the journey to and from your establishment
  - In the garden
  - Going shopping

- When parents stay on at nursery to volunteer, include maths play in their jobs – perhaps helping children to play a game outside that involves scoring and recording.

- Develop a bank of outdoor mathematical games which parents can borrow. Kick-start this with an open session in your class so that everyone gets a chance to share, play and enjoy the games – there are lots in this book.

There are multicultural variations of many games and even within the UK there are different regional versions. Take time to celebrate this diversity and add suggestions made by parents to your bank of games.

Whilst book bags or story sacks are popular in many education and childcare settings, maths kits and games are less common. This is a missed opportunity to develop children's mathematical skills and competences. In particular, games and challenges give parents and children an opportunity to spend quality time together.

There are lots of experiences and games which can be shared with parents in each chapter. Many of the suggestions do not involve educational props but use ordinary household items.

Last year, I introduced 'treasure bags'. The children each printed handprints onto their bag. It belongs to them – they already have ownership of it. I attached a laminated poem to each bag:

> If I go for a walk, what will Mother Nature leave for me?
>
> If I go to the beach, what treasures will the sea wash ashore?
>
> If I go to the woods, what will the winds blow in?
>
> What will the fairies sprinkle or the giants drop?
>
> I'll **POP** them into my bag!

After the weekend or after a weekday walk, the children would bring their bag back to the setting full of precious items which are special to them (leaves, stones, sticks, shells, seaweed, etc.). What an abundance of fantastic objects, just bursting with mathematical possibilities! Another bonus is that such objects helped to resource the outdoor space.

Rachel Besford, nursery teacher, Little Explorers Outdoor Pre-School, Cornwall

Idea 2.5 | Seeking out and using natural environments

In recent years there has been a rapid rise in the number of outdoor nurseries and similar settings where children spend almost all their time outside in natural spaces such as woods, beaches and parkland. Nature is the resource and context for all curriculum areas. The natural world provides a creative mathematical environment which extends provision rather than restricts it.

When children play in a space or with an object they experience it in a unique way. They view it in terms of its 'affordances' rather than its common or predetermined use. The affordances of an object or space are all the things it has the potential to do or be. Natural spaces have a high level of affordance. A feature such as a fallen log could be a balance beam, a crocodile, a site to find mini-beasts, a place to sit, the setting for role play and much more. On top of natural features such as logs, boulders and water sources, there is an abundance of natural 'loose parts' such as stones, sticks, cones and shells. The possibilities are considerable and therefore the mathematical opportunities are endless.

> As a dedicated outdoor educator it is my job to see and unlock the learning potential of the forest. Under the umbrella of 'maths' there are so many opportunities if you take the time to look. Some of my personal favourites are as simple as folding leaves to look at fractions, laying out leaves to look at patterns, collecting firewood which helps with grouping, quantities and measurements, and den building which helps with proportions, positional language, estimates, three-dimensional construction and measurements.
>
> Alice Buckley, Nature to Nurture Outdoor Nursery, Croxteth Country Park, Liverpool

My professional perception and practice of maths has been totally changed by working with natural materials outside. When I started teaching in the early 1990s I would have regarded the whole idea as interesting but wacky. I probably would have found a way of hanging a set of shapes from trees or painted numbers onto tarps to convince myself I was 'doing' maths properly, even if the children took little notice of my efforts.

Resources

I believe that a mathematically rich environment is created by ensuring that children have the freedom to play, investigate, question and experiment with their ideas using open-ended resources that have no fixed way of being used. These are often referred to as 'loose parts' and include:

- Natural resources such as sticks and stones.
- Man-made materials: household junk, scrap and repurposed materials.
- Materials found *in situ*: sand, water, snow, mud, gravel, plant matter as well as random found objects.
- Specific maths resources.

When a child discovers a stick, stone or other resource in the environment and uses it in their play, a personal connection is fostered with that object. Give the children time to do this with all resources. Observing children using an object in their play will help you to work out the mathematical input that is needed (as discussed in Chapter 1). The use of loose parts helps the children to learn that maths is all around us. It also demonstrates a professional commitment to the sustainable and wise use of resources.

Gathering and creating resources with children makes them meaningful. It can help to reinforce our connectedness to nature and our sense of place. Remember to check the by-laws and land access rights of your country when collecting natural materials. Follow any collection codes that exist and only take a little at a time.

Idea 2.6 Caring for your resources

Specific maths resources need to be clearly labelled or presented in such a way so that the children can easily find out what is available and know where everything belongs. Time needs to be spent developing routines along with clear, positive expectations that the resources which require looking after will be returned to their rightful place.

Idea 2.7 : The really useful resource list

■ **Light-coloured cloth:** Useful for being able to see gathered resources. Put a blank 100 square on the reverse to use for additional mathematical games of different sorts.

■ **Number sets:** There are lots of different number sets available for outdoor use which can be bought or made. Examples include mirror numbers, wooden numbers, numbered skittles, different types of dice, painted number pebbles, 0–9 in lots of different colours, heavy duty tiles and large 0–100 wooden slices.

■ **Fluorescent cards:** Have these in different colours (e.g. green, yellow, orange, pink) with the digits 0–9 on each colour. This allows for team games, trails and hunts following specific colours. They are visually attractive on dull days and draw the children's attention to the numbers. Peg two or more digits together to create numbers beyond 9, thereby beginning to introduce the concept of place value.

■ **Number lines:** Have a variety of number lines, including blank tracks so that numbers can be written on them as needed (see Ideas 3.17, 3.18 and 3.26).

■ **Mathematical print:** Examples include old calendars – perpetual calendars never go out of date; part of a phone book; old computer keyboards – remove the cables first; old mobile phones – remove the battery and reseal; recipe cards; shopping receipts; bus, plane and train tickets; and catalogues of different sorts – DIY, car, outdoor sports and gardening catalogues are particularly relevant for outside.

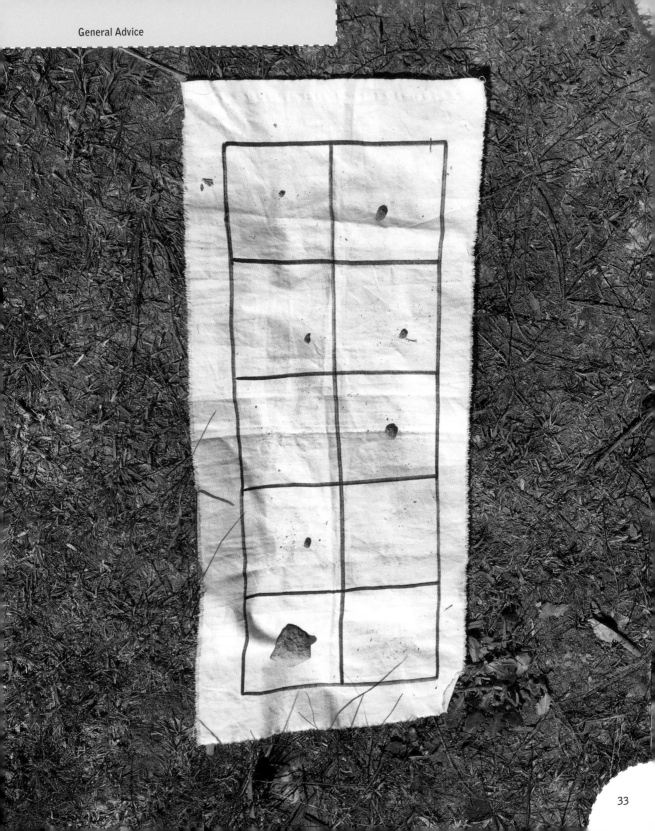

■ **Arrays:** These are fixed arrangements of rows and columns which can be helpful for laying out objects. Ice cube trays, muffin trays and egg boxes are good examples. Concepts such as conservation of number, counting in groups and the number functions can all be explored using arrays. Put outline grids on tarps or plain cotton sheets for sorting free and found treasures and finds. Tens frames are particularly useful arrays.

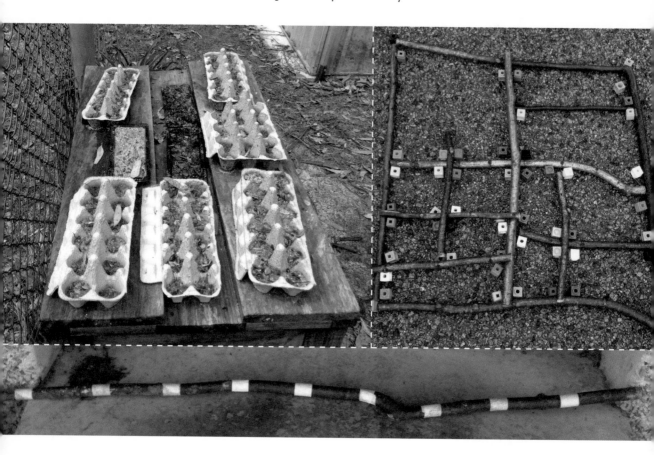

■ **Cut sticks:** Develop a collection of sticks cut to specific lengths: 1 metre, 90 cm, 80 cm down to 10 cm or 5 cm. These can be used to represent, order and manipulate numbers in different ways. They are also valuable for exploring length. Colour-code the ends to help with quick identification. Also useful are 25 cm and 33.3 cm, for fraction investigations.

■ **One metre measuring stick:**[2] Mark 10 cm intervals on a one metre stick. It is useful for rounding to the nearest ten and quick estimates, such as how deep is a puddle, how wide is

---

2 See J. Robertson, Measuring sticks, *Creative Star Learning* (20 October 2011). Available at: http://creativestarlearning.co.uk/maths-outdoors/measuring-sticks/.

a door, how long is a path or how high is our sunflower. The intervals can be counted in tens or ones, depending on the child's level of understanding. It also makes a useful lead stick on a walk – whoever is at the front holds the stick.

- **Large wooden items:** Tree stumps can be cut to specific heights, although avoid making them too tall, usually 50 cm is sufficient. Planks of wood are also good to have in specific lengths such as 1 metre, 50 cm and 25 cm. This provides a set of construction resources which can be used for many different practical calculations.

- **Rope:** Have different lengths, colours, widths and textures. Ropes serve a similar purpose to cut sticks but are flexible and so are useful for measuring and working with wiggly lines and objects with curved sides. A large rope with marks at one metre intervals is useful for large-scale measuring and creating group circles quickly.

- **Measuring time:** Use sand-timers that measure a range of times, stopwatches and clocks (digital and analogue) and cameras to capture seasonal changes that take place over time.

- **Two-dimensional shapes and three-dimensional objects:** Build up a collection of standard and non-standard cubes, cuboids, cylinders, cones and pyramids from unwanted junk (e.g. collect tins of different sorts). Snack boxes usually come in many different shapes and sizes and are ideal for this purpose. If you have any old collections or odd bits and pieces of two- and three-dimensional shapes which have been used indoors then these can have their shelf life extended outside.

- **Maths tarp:** Once an old tarp becomes worn, give it a new lease of life by cutting out a range of shapes. Use for peek-a-boo or posting games, den building, picnics and so on.

- **PE equipment:** Cones, bean bags, discs and hoops are useful items in that they often have clear attributes which work well for pattern investigations as well as shape, position and data-handling work.

- **Pocket-sized resources:** These items are useful for keeping in your pocket as you go about your daily work:

  - A one metre piece of thin rope (see Idea 2.1)

  - A miniature sand-timer

- A digital device with various built-in apps like a compass, stop-watch and calculator
- A small, retractable tape measure
- A miniature number line that can be rolled up
- A pair of dice
- A notebook and pencil
- Pocket-sized prompt cards (see Idea 1.5)
- A finger puppet such as a mouse or other British wildlife creature (see Idea 2.1)
- A number fan which provides the number names, digits and dots

■ **For packing and transporting materials:** Old suitcases, small trolleys, baskets, trays, bread crates, buckets, fish crates, trailers and pulleys. These are useful for position and movement work as well as exploring capacity and three-dimensional space.

■ **Non-standard tools for measuring:**
- Spoons, scoops, shovels, pipettes, turkey basters, ladles
- Different lengths and diameters of hoses, tubes, ropes, washing line, string, old bandages, masking tape, skipping ropes, guttering and pipes, ribbons[3]
- Items to help fill containers such as hand-held pumps, water pumps, funnels, watering cans, teapots
- Bucket or balance scales

■ **Standardised containers and resources in a range of sizes (e.g. 1 litre, 500 ml, 250 ml):**
- Milk bottles, ice cream tubs, toiletry containers such as shampoo bottles, plastic tubs, tablespoons, teaspoons
- Sticks and rope cut to a variety of standardised lengths (e.g. 1 metre, 50 cm), trundle wheels

■ **Resources with scale marks:**
- Measuring jugs, syringes, measuring cups, measuring cylinders
- Standardised weights and balance scales
- Tape measures, metre sticks
- Old-fashioned kitchen scales with weights

---

3 There are many posts on my website which discuss the play value and possibilities of these resources. Please check them out at: www.creativestarlearning.co.uk. Also remember that resources may need to be included in your risk–benefit assessment of your outdoor space (e.g. the use of ropes).

■ **General resource advice:**

○ Keep the labels on containers for as long as possible so the children can see the link between the container and its numerical capacity.

○ Go miniature – link into small world play and use for working off-site when mass and size become critical. Conversely, giant-sized resources help children to explore their strength, as well as embody the learning and aid cooperation.

○ Develop collections of different objects. These help children to sort and classify objects according to many different attributes and engage in mathematical discussions.

Mathematical symbols and mark making

Mathematical mark making includes all the symbols that represent children's mathematical thinking. It may appear as random marks on the ground, prints, outlines or other graphics, or as attempts at forming standard notations such as numerals, symbols and shapes.

What matters is that the marks make sense to the child who made them. As educators, our job is to recognise and value these marks. We engage with the child to find out more and facilitate discussions and thinking about the mathematical concepts that the marks represent. They are a bridge from the child's concrete experiences to representing these through the use of symbols. The marks demonstrate connections in their thinking.

Mark making should be initiated and led by each individual child as part of their play at a time when they are interested and ready. A formal introduction to writing numbers and other mathematical symbols should not be necessary, and indeed can be counterproductive in that they may make no sense to a child who is not ready for the 'abstract symbolism of school-based mathematics'.[4]

Being outside allows for different ways of engaging in mathematical mark making. Whilst natural habitats may not seem obvious places for the physical act of recording numbers and mathematical outputs, they are a rich source of stimuli. There are multiple

---

4 M. Worthington and E. Carruthers, Becoming bi-numerate: a study of teachers' practices concerning children's early 'written' mathematics. Paper presented at the European Early Childhood Education Research Association (EECERA) conference, University of Strathclyde, 4–7 September 2003. Available at: http://childrens-mathematics.net/paper_teachers-practices.pdf, p. 2.

surfaces available, from the bark of trees to smooth stones, snow and sand. Tools can be created from found materials – for example, using charcoal left over from a fire the day before or simply picking up and using a stick. The weather and seasons provide constant variation.

There are three approaches to mathematical mark making which help to inform our observations of children:

1   Independent scribbles of numerals, symbols and marks. Always praise children's efforts and encourage individuals to read their efforts aloud or explain what they have recorded. The focus in discussions needs to be on what these mathematical graphics represent. Only focus on correct formation and layout if this is important to the child.

2   Scribing numbers in a way that actively involves the children. Talk aloud about how you are forming the numbers as you scribe them and ask the children to check your work for accuracy. Ensure that what you have scribed is fit for the child's purpose. Your scribing needs to be child, not adult, directed.

3   Copying – this might be other children's work or numbers seen in the environment. You may wish to have a laminated set of numbers that the children can use as models or to lay natural materials on top of them. Once they are confident doing this, the children can use the cards to copy. Eventually they will be able to write formal symbols from memory.

You need to carefully consider where you can make links or introduce mathematical mark-making opportunities in different activities and areas outside, such as role play, physical activities, construction and so on.

Idea 2.8 Embedding mathematical mark making into routines

Here are some ideas for getting the children familiar with mathematical notation:

■   Write mathematical symbols as part of the information about an outdoor snack.

■   Encourage the children to put a tick on a chart to indicate a preference.

■   Involve children in planning which includes maps, symbols and numbers.

■   Label outdoor clothing and coat pegs using numbers.

■   Keep scores and mark make when playing games. Adults can model this initially but encourage the children to take on this role.

■   Note the weather, temperature and date on a weather chart.

■   Use data-handling experiences as mathematical mark-making opportunities (see Chapter 11).

Idea 2.9   Mark-making props

Mark-making resources need to be considered in terms of the development of the fine and gross motor skills needed to improve coordination, such as big and small movements or those which require different types of grip.[5] Some ideas to consider include:

- Use chalk or water on walls, pavements and asphalt. Remember to only use chalk in places where it is acceptable to do so and won't cause public offence.

- Water-based resources: plastic syringes of different sizes; different sized brushes from tiny shaving brushes to big brooms; pipettes, pumps and turkey basters; water pistols; funnels; bottles with holes; washing-up liquid bottles; pump action spray bottles.

- Mud and sand areas benefit from rakes, spades, sticks, scrapers, cones and other resources that can mark or change the surface of the mud or sand.

- Put slates, small whiteboards, acrylic mirrors and small pieces of Perspex in different places outside with relevant mark-making materials to write on these portable surfaces.

- A variety of different sized clipboards are useful. A3 is especially good for big writing and notices. The larger size is easier for children with fine motor difficulties to manage. A5 clipboards are great for small places where just little messages, notes and marks need to be made. Use scoreboards and clipboards for games. Boxboard can be cut to size to make informal clipboards.

---

5 A useful book for developing mark making is Alistair Bryce-Clegg's *50 Fantastic Ideas for Mark Making* (London: Featherstone Education, 2015).

- Scrap pieces of cardboard work well outside. Big pieces of paper can get soggy and flap about in the wind.

- Natural resources: feathers, stones and sticks. These can be writing implements as well as writing surfaces.

Idea 2.10 | Developing number formation

According to Sian Eckersley, a paediatric occupational therapist, 'The child's stages of development and "readiness" for handwriting need to be taken into consideration.'[6] Eckersley sums up the consensus from research, reporting that teaching children handwriting before they are ready has been found to create difficulties with writing that are hard to reconcile later. Children won't generally be ready for formal handwriting practice until they are aged 5 or 6. Prior to this their visual, sensory, motor and perceptual systems will not be integrated to the level required to form letters.

Here are some examples of outdoor activities to undertake with a child who is developmentally ready but has not yet put pencil to paper:

- Sticky numbers. Create 'sticky' numbers by rolling out a length of clay which is pressed onto a sheet of card. The children stick natural materials into the clay slab to create the number.

- Natural numbers. Make a number from natural materials such as weeds, sticks or stones, then take a photo of it *in situ* before it gets destroyed. Materials can be stuck onto many surfaces using mud or clay.

- Three-dimensional numbers. Make these in the sandpit or on a beach, from mud, clay, snow or any malleable material.

- Stick numbers. Every child likes finding a stick and using it. This works well informally when out and about beyond your outdoor space.

---

6 S. Eckersley, Handwriting, *Occupational Therapy for Children* (22 February 2011). Available at: http://occupationaltherapyforchildren.over-blog.com/article-handwriting-67838149.html.

Different sizes of stick affect the movements made, and it is a natural progression from using a finger.

- ○ Form numbers in puddles by swirling the stick.

- ○ Use the stick to draw numbers in sand, mud, grit, etc. What is the biggest number possible which can be made in the space available?

- ○ Use the stick to air-write numbers. Attach ribbons or string for added effect.

- ○ Make numerals using little twigs.

Problem-solving and reasoning

Problem-solving happens naturally outside as the weather, seasons and environment provide lots of challenges. For instance, on a windy day, the children may have to find a way of working that stops their materials from blowing away. An object may be thrown onto a roof accidentally and the children may have to work out how to retrieve it. A small stream is suddenly too wide and deep to cross after heavy rain, so they may have to think about an alternative way of reaching their destination.

By the time a child is three years old, they will be adept at problem-solving. Think about the effort that goes into learning how to walk. We naturally want to assist children but this can sometimes hamper their ability to work out a solution. When a child falls over, it is tempting to help them back onto their feet. If we let the child work out how to pick themselves up and dust themselves down, then this helps them to become more independent and confident. We can hug and praise them for getting up and getting going afterwards.

All the skills required in day-to-day problem-solving can be developed, used and applied in maths. Practitioners will need to consider how to frame mathematically probing questions and comments when working with or alongside children. This takes concerted effort and practice to develop. It usually begins with stepping back, observing and waiting before choosing to intervene – if at all. You can always take a photo quietly and later ask the child to tell you more about what they were doing and the strategies they were using to solve a problem.

Idea 2.11 | Every moment is a problem-solving moment

Take a close look at the routines in your setting and tweak them to ensure that the children have to make decisions and think for themselves. This can be as simple as ensuring the children prepare and wear their own backpacks for an off-site visit. Try the following strategies:

- Enable the children to discover the answer rather than supplying it. Don't be afraid to leave a problem unsolved and return to it another time or day. Real problems take real amounts of time to sort – not everything is a quick fix.

- Start with what the children already know, then build on the knowledge by asking questions which stretch their thinking or encourage them to explain what they have done and why. Have a look at some of the prompts in Idea 2.14.

- Encourage the children to see that problems can be solved in many ways. Acknowledge all solutions and different ways of thinking about a problem.

- Invite collaboration amongst the children. If one child is unsure then perhaps another child or group can advise. Involve all the children, not just the most able.

Idea 2.12 | Using natural materials to stimulate problem-solving and higher order thinking

The non-uniformity of natural materials often requires us to think harder and in more divergent ways. This can be illustrated by finding a leaf and tearing it into five pieces. Give your torn-up leaf to a colleague and ask them to put it back together.

Compare this task to completing a manufactured wooden five-piece jigsaw. As well as being a lot cheaper, the leaf is a much more challenging task. There's no picture to look at, and it can be hard to discriminate between the natural and torn edges or work out which way up the leaf should be.

Idea 2.13 : Building a collaborative community by group problem-solving

Look for real life situations where children can naturally problem-solve. It is very empowering for them and it helps to create a stronger sense of community in which every child has a voice and their opinions are valued.

For example, if there is a problem with tidying away resources, encourage the group to think about why this is a problem – write down their suggestions. Next, encourage the children to come up with ideas for solving the problem. These can also be written down. It can be helpful to get the children to act out the suggestions and to prompt them to think about what everyone will be doing and saying. This can help a child or group to articulate their thoughts and it makes the ideas more real. It is also an opportunity to highlight and explain some problem-solving language.

After further discussion with the group, try one or two of their suggested strategies. Even if you think a suggestion is unworkable, let the children give it a go. After a few days, review the success of the strategy. What worked well? What would be even better? Does the strategy need to be ditched and a new one from the list tried? Continue this experimental approach until the problem has been solved.

Idea 2.14 | Pocket-sized prompt sheets

These prompts are especially useful if you are twitching to intervene. Keep calm and look for the problem-solving strategies being used before offering prompts, which may include the following:

Describing prompts – say aloud what you see the children doing

- Breaking the problem into smaller parts.
- Acting out an idea.
- Looking for a pattern.
- Estimating and then checking in order to improve.
- Working backwards.

Reasoning prompts – I wonder if you could try …?

- A simpler way.
- Working with others.
- Doing one thing at a time.
- Looking for a pattern.

Recording the process – why not …?

- Draw a picture or diagram of what you did or what you want the outcome to be.
- Make a model.
- Produce an organised list.

(See also the data-handling ideas in Chapter 11.)

Deepening the learning prompts

- What worked well?
- What would you do differently next time?
- How did you feel when …?

- Does this remind you of anything else you have done before?
- It would be useful if you could tell X what you did.

Idea 2.15 Estimating everything

Children need lots of practice at estimating so they are able to make reasoned estimates based upon experience and knowledge rather than wild guesses. It is a basic strategy for problem-solving and enquiry work as well as a useful life skill.

Being outside provides a real context for estimating. It is hard to tell the number of birds in a flock or bricks in a wall, or exactly how long it will take to walk to the shops, so there is a constant need to make estimates of amounts based upon our experiences.

Practitioners can bring estimation into discussions in an incidental way and encourage the children to make estimates.

- Number: having a guess before counting the number of fence posts at the end of a field.
- Money: evaluating whether we have enough money to buy something we need.
- Distance: estimating how far away the nearest shop is.
- Volume: thinking about the volume of water in one bucket compared to another.
- Shape: estimating the number of vertices on a cuboid before finding a systematic way of counting them.
- Weight and mass: wondering how much food the birds will eat.
- Time: considering how long it will take for a pine cone to close when soaked with water.

The children will be making assessments about a lot of different matters in their play. When observing children, listen and look for evidence of their ability to estimate (e.g. talking about how many more bricks are needed to make a tower, telling another person how far they can kick or throw a ball, thinking about whether it is possible to walk all the way along a narrow fallen tree trunk). Being able to make a reasonable guess is an indication of their understanding of number and quantity.

When children make unrealistic estimations about quantities, such as there being millions of shells in a basket, be aware that they are playing with number words which mean a really large quantity to them. This is a great conversation starter that can lead to more explorations of big numbers (as discussed in Idea 3.31).

Estimation involves conversations. Adults can model lines of thought and ways of making a reasonable guess. You need to reinforce that a correct answer is not necessary. This often works best when an exact answer is not known or cannot be determined. A good tactic is to get a group to make a joint estimation so that no one person is right or wrong.

The children had planted peas and they were ready to harvest. I encouraged the children to pick the peas but first they had to estimate how many they thought might be inside the pods. The children loved the surprise element of guessing how many peas were inside. Some recorded their guesses with chalk on a log. Some had a go at writing the numeral and then counting to see how many. We talked about whether the estimate was a good guess. Who had more? Fewer? Fewest? There was lots of language about the size of the peas. We found the total number of peas in two pods. One simple activity produced a lot of discussions.

Rachel Besford, nursery teacher, Little Explorers Outdoor Pre-School, Cornwall

CHAPTER 3

Exploring Numbers

This chapter is about counting, sorting, matching, ordering and recognising numbers. We use numbers in our everyday lives without giving much thought to what a number represents. A number is a symbol. It can be expressed as a numeral or in word form to represent several different concepts.

Children need to have lots of experiences of cardinal, ordinal and nominal numbers. Within one period of time, it is quite possible for children to use numbers in all these forms in their play without distinguishing between the different types. Whilst addition, subtraction and other number processes are discussed in Chapter 4, these are inextricably linked to the skills, knowledge and understanding of number that is covered here.

Cardinal numbers

A cardinal number represents the quantity of an object, so 1 = one object, 2 = two objects, etc. They do not include fractions, decimals or percentages, only whole numbers. Children need to be able to match the correct number of objects to the number symbol and rearrange groups of objects, or change the order in which they are counted, to understand that the total will not change and that the number of objects is conserved.

Ordinal numbers

An ordinal number tells us about the position and order of objects, so first, second, third, etc. It is also about the order and position of numbers in relation to each other. It is about 2 always being one more than 3, or 5 always being in-between 4 and 6. Street numbers are ordinal, and so are the numbers on an analogue clock and the pages in a book.

The language of position is essential to understanding the ordinal aspect of numbers. Children need to know and understand that when counting, 'one more than' is always the next number to be counted. Likewise, 'one less than' refers to the previous number which has been counted. This can be surprisingly tricky for children to understand.

Children need plenty of experiences of counting ordinal numbers. It is just as important as counting groups of objects. The concept that a number can represent a point or position is as important as knowing that a symbol such as 7, and the word 'seven', represents a set of seven objects.

One advantage of counting ordinal numbers outside is that the position of objects does not matters – that is, whether a group of objects is in a line, cluster or other pattern or whether you count up or down, left or right is irrelevant. What is important is that one-to-one correspondence occurs. Every object is given a number name and the sequence is prescribed: 1, 2, 3, etc. Whatever the layout or arrangement of the objects, the number is conserved.

Nominal numbers

A nominal number has neither value nor position. Examples include postcodes, numbers on the backs of team players (e.g. on rugby shirts) and Thomas the Tank Engine's number. What makes these numbers unique is that they could be replaced by a different symbol altogether. For example, in the game of hockey, players used to wear their positions on their shirts rather than a number.

As adults we need to have an understanding of the purpose of numbers and what they represent. On your way to or from work, have a look at the numbers you see, or have a look around your house. Try to categorise them into cardinal, ordinal and nominal numbers. Do you find it easier to identify one category than another? Are there any numbers which you are not sure about? If so, see what others think. Mathematics is about asking these sorts of questions and exploring puzzles like this.

When introducing number concepts, make sure the children have lots of time to play, experiment and have fun with numbers, particularly in their free play. Structured games and experiences are most effective when the children indicate an interest. For this reason, the suggestions in this section are deliberately open-ended so they can be readily adapted to a child's current interest or ongoing passion. There are a number of general rules of thumb when developing number skills and concepts as outlined in Ideas 3.1 to 3.4.

Vocabulary

After, before, bigger, count back, count on, count up to, digits, even, fewer, fives, hundreds, in-between, least, less, match, more, most, next, numbers, numerals, odd, one less than, one more than, ones, order, place value, previous, recognise, sort, tens, units, what's missing

Expressions

A stitch in time saves nine

A bird in the hand is worth two in the bush

Counting your blessings

Idea 3.1 Thinking beyond 1 to 10

Play and have fun with big numbers too. If a child can count from 1 to 10 then they can count from 1,000 to 10,000 in thousands or from 1 million through to 10 million and beyond. Children will notice big numbers in their local environment and at home. When this happens it is something to build upon, not ignore. Their understanding of place value will come in due course and will often arise spontaneously in play.[1]

---

1 A lovely account of place value explorations in nursery can be seen in this blog post: C. Dunn, Racing to understand place value in EYFS, *Mr Shrek* (9 May 2013). Available at: http://mr-shrek.blogspot.co.uk/2013/05/racing-to-understand-place-value-in-eyfs. html?spref=tw&m=1.

Idea 3.2 Counting backwards as well as forwards

Children find counting backwards more challenging than counting forwards, yet it is a necessary skill for understanding subtraction. They will first become confident with a sequence they have frequently repeated, such as counting back from 10 to 0. Even if they know this they may still find it challenging to count back from a different number within that chain (e.g. when asked to count back from 8 they will want to start from 10), but this will develop as they become more confident. Quick ways include:

- Counting forwards when climbing up steps and counting backwards when walking down steps.

- Counting down to start a race.

- 3, 2, 1 … and lift off! – going into space in a rocket.

- Using big movements such as taking steps, jumps or hops when counting – for example, when jumping forwards, count forwards, and when jumping backwards, count backwards.

Idea 3.3 Counting objects for a reason, not just for the sake of counting

It takes a bit of discipline on the part of the practitioner to make sure objects are being counted for a reason, as it is easy to slip into the habit of counting anything and everything. This has the potential to disrupt play, so be mindful of this and only intervene with counting if it matters to the children you are working with.

Often comparative counting is a friendly approach. For example:

- If there are five jackets hanging on a peg, ask if there are enough for every child in the group.

- During role play, ask for a certain number of items and then ask for one more, explaining why this has made a difference.

Idea 3.4 One-to-one matching of number names to objects

Matching number names to objects is an important skill to learn – being able to move your finger to touch an object and count aloud. You have to keep track of what you have counted as well as know which objects still need to be counted.

There are different skills involved in counting. For example:

- Counting aloud the numbers in order.

- Touching or moving objects as they are counted.

- Counting without touching objects but by seeing them.

- Counting without visual prompts.

- Transferring counting skills from one context to another, such as a different place or type of object.

- Being able to count objects laid out in different ways (e.g. line, circle, heap, scattered objects).

- Recognising small quantities of objects (e.g. one to three items) without the need to count them. This is called subitising. With familiar patterns such as dice and dominoes, children can recognise larger values instantly.

- Doing all of the above but gradually extending to counting objects in groups of twos, fives and tens. This is significantly more challenging and should be undertaken when a relevant opportunity arises, such as counting pairs of socks or wellies or gathering sticks for making a fire into bundles of ten.

Idea 3.5 Maths trees

A number tree serves as a great conversation piece. It is a branch stuck into a bucket of earth or a small tree or shrub growing in your outdoor space. Hang different numbers on the tree and change these often to keep the tree a focal point. For example:

- Hang the same number all over the tree.

- Hang just two numbers on the tree.

- Put out numbers bigger than ten.

- Create an advent tree. The children can take turns to add or remove a number in order during the lead-up to Christmas. This can work for any special occasion.

- Ask everyone's favourite number and reason why: write these on luggage tags to hang up.

Alternatively, let the children chose numbers to decorate the tree with and encourage them to give reasons for their choices. If they are unable to explain their choice, then others can have fun guessing what the pattern or number choice is. When talking about the numbers on the tree, a simple question such as, 'What is the same about these numbers?' or 'What is different about these numbers?' can lead to all sorts of conversations and reasoning.

Learning to estimate numbers

(See notes on estimation in Chapter 2.)

Idea 3.6 Estimation jars

Create an estimation jar for the children to play with outside. The children fill it with objects of their choosing such as pebbles or cones. The group or a child has to estimate how many objects are in the jar before counting them.

Idea 3.7 Direct comparisons

When the children are filling containers such as milk bottles or transparent tubes with stones or gravel, this is an opportunity for them to estimate and count. Challenge the child or group to release half the amount of stones and count them. This can then become the basis for estimating the amount of stones left in the bottle. These can then be removed and counted.

Idea 3.8 Sand sculpture bottles

This is a fun thing to do during a visit to the beach. The group needs a plastic bottle or a transparent container. Any interesting things they find can be put into the bottle, such as little bits of driftwood or shells. Next, the children should half-fill their bottle with dry sand and put the top back on. They can then have fun estimating what is inside the bottle and in what quantity (e.g. three shells, two pebbles, five pieces of sea glass and one driftwood stick).

Idea 3.9 Leafleting

For this autumnal activity, you need to have access to trees or plants with compound leaves. For example, horse chestnut (*Aesculus hippocastanum*) leaves have five leaflets coming off the stem; however, others, like ash (*Fraxinus excelsior*), have a variable quantity of leaflets. A good game can be had by showing a group of children a compound leaf for a few seconds, hiding it behind your back, then asking them to estimate the number of leaflets on the stem. Once everyone has given their estimate, bring the leaf out and together count the leaflets as you point to them.

Older children can play this game in pairs once it has been modelled. They can collect different leaves with different numbers of leaflets for this purpose. A variation is to estimate and then count the number of black spots on sycamore (*Acer pseudoplatanus*) leaves. This is tar fungus and is harmless.

Counting, ordering and recognising numbers

Idea 3.10 Find a number

If the children have been finding and collecting different objects outside, such as cones or sticks, ask each child to put their collection in front of them in the gathering circle. Then call out different actions such as:

- Sit down if you have fewer than four objects.

- Swap places with someone if you have only one object.

- Stand on one leg if you have between three and seven objects.

- Find someone with the same object and find the total number of both of your objects.

- Share your objects equally with a friend.

Once the children understand the game, they can also call out instructions.

Idea 3.11 The big outdoor number book

The creation of a book of shared thoughts and ideas around different aspects of maths allows for lots of formal and informal discussions about the mathematical world in which we live. Each page can contain a range of illustrations. For example, for the number three the children may find:

- Sets of three (e.g. three pressed leaves, a photo of three items).

- An example of the number 3 found in the environment (e.g. on a door).

- Photos of other ways of writing three (e.g. Roman numerals, 1p and 2p coins).

- Page 3 indicated in a book.

- Interesting number facts about three (e.g. $3 = 2 + 1$).

- A range of simple challenges linked to the number, such as 'What do you see on the ground when you take just three steps outside?'

- Reasons to like this number, based upon conversations or interviews with other people.

Parents can also help the children to collect and identify numbers. Many children also like to make little pocket number books. These can move between home and school.

Idea 3.12 : Our plant book

This book is a variation of Idea 3.11. It enables children to develop their counting skills when looking closely at plants. When the children pick a weed or common flower these can be examined to see which number page the plant could be added to.[2] For example, clover has three leaves so this could represent the number three. Alternatively, any four leaves from one tree species could be used to represent the number four.

When children are investigating plants, hand out magnifying lenses or glasses to encourage them to look more closely at the natural objects and plants. A single leaf may have one stem, two colours, three chew holes or ten veins! Leaves and plants can be pressed between cardboard and clipboards to help keep their colour and shape.[3] Once the objects are dry and flat, the children can glue them into their outdoor counting books. These can be read and reread as often as wanted.

---

2 Common weeds are perfectly acceptable to pick in moderation. For further guidance, have a look at the Wild Flower Society's code of conduct: http://www.thewildflowersociety.com/wfs_new_pages/1f_code_of_conduct.htm.

3 For instructions on how to do this, have a look at this blog post: J. Robertson, DIY clipboard flower press, *Creative Star Learning* (14 May 2015). Available at: http://creativestarlearning.co.uk/early-years-outdoors/diy-clipboard-flower-press/.

Idea 3.13 Skittles

As the children set up the skittles, they can count the number of skittles present. When a knockout happens and all the skittles get scattered, the children can gather, count and check that the correct number are still present. Encourage the children to reposition the skittles in different ways of their choosing. This helps them to understand that the number of objects is conserved in spite of the different layout or formation.

Idea 3.14 Picture sticks

This challenge generates a lot of discussion about the conservation of number. The children collect an agreed number of sticks – for example, each child goes and finds ten sticks and brings them back to the gathering circle. The challenge is for each child to make a picture with their ten sticks. Everyone can step back and comment on the different pictures created.

You may need to put a size limit on the sticks and request that each stick should be no bigger than a hand, unless you are happy with huge sticks and branches coming back to the circle!

This activity can be easily extended to any number of objects. It is a very enjoyable way of counting objects for a purpose – for example, try creating 'twenty object' pictures where there must be twenty of any object used.

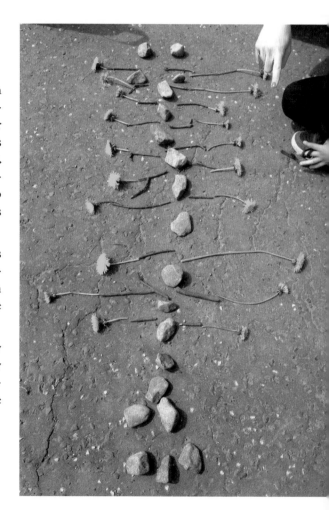

Idea 3.15 Petra's dice pattern game

Petra Jäger, founder of the first Waldkindergarten – forest nursery – in Germany, showed me this game, which is a favourite with her children. You need six pebbles. Throw some, but not all, of the pebbles on the ground. The children estimate how many there are. Next, count them together. Then one child puts them into the layout of a dice pattern. Everyone checks to see if this is correct. Older children often want to use twelve pebbles to make two dice and are able to partition the numbers correctly. This helps with their addition skills.

Idea 3.16 Fill the hole

This game can be adapted to any hole dug anywhere. If a child digs a hole, then it needs to be filled with objects until it is full. This tends to happen spontaneously and is a lot of fun! Usually other children join in.

Encourage the children to count the number of objects that are being flung into the hole. Model writing down the numbers to keep a record. You can also try introducing the concept of counting on from the previous number as the children bring up different objects to drop into the hole. At the end you have a filled hole. If it contains resources which need to be put away then ask the children to take the items out of the hole. Count them and sort them as this is done.

If you come across a hole when out and about, always remember to check if an animal lives there. They will not like things being shoved into their hole. Do this activity with fresh child-dug holes only.

Idea 3.17 Environmental number lines

A number line is helpful as a visual aid for children to be able to see the relationship of one number to another, as is looking at the movement of a finger or object when counting forwards and backwards. Lines can be horizontal or vertical, and numbers can be added if needed.

There are variations of number lines which can be used for counting when working outside. For example:

- Pavement slabs

- Fence posts

- A line of lamp posts or avenue of trees that are evenly spaced out

- Bricks in a wall

- Lines made by children, such as a line of sticks, stones or pebbles

- Rope with tags at regular intervals (e.g. one metre apart)

- One metre measuring sticks (as described in Idea 2.7)

Idea 3.18 Pocket number lines

Make yourself some little rolled up number strips which can be carried in a pocket. The children can use them to:

- Reinforce the order of numbers by counting forwards and backwards. As a child counts, encourage them to touch each number.

- Talk about the number before and after (thus linking to addition and subtraction through the concept of 'one more than' and 'one less than').

- Help match found objects to the numbers on the strip.

- Match number cards to the numbers on the strip.

A blank number strip is also useful. The children can:

- Choose which numbers are put on the strip. It is not necessary to begin at zero or one.

- Lay out the numbers horizontally or vertically and experience the act of creating each type of number line.

- Decide whether the numbers should be placed in the spaces between the lines or just below the marked lines. Children need experience of both ways of displaying and counting objects as they serve different purposes.

Idea 3.19 Stick tapping

At a gathering circle, using sticks or stones to tap along to the beat of a song is an entry point into counting games. From here, move on to activities such as counting forwards whilst slowly tapping one stick on the ground in time to each number said aloud. Encourage all the children to join in with counting aloud. Work on developing a steady rhythm. Variations include:

- Count on from different numbers – let the children choose the starting point.

- Count backwards as often as forwards – this helps with subtraction.

- Develop a 'switch' and challenge the children to begin by counting forwards and then when someone calls out 'switch', you change direction and count backwards.

- Use two sticks and tap with alternate sticks on the ground.

- Pass the tapping sticks around a circle – this can be linked to songs and keeping a beat.

- Stand up and tap using one metre sticks with older children.

For each approach – tapping, passing or listening – start simple and build up the complexity in line with what your children can manage and where they are developmentally. A little and often approach works well.

Idea 3.20 | Hopscotch

Use hopscotch layouts for number activities. Have a look at online images of grids from different countries and cultures and encourage the children to invent their own. Pavements in quiet streets can be used too, so encourage parents and carers to play this game with their child.

The extensions below help children to understand and gain confidence when talking about and using numbers. You could try:

- Finding objects outside and putting the correct quantities in each square.

- Playing hopscotch in different ways – change the rules.

- Taking it in turns to cover up the numbers for others to guess which one is underneath.

- Using dice which have 'one more than' or 'one less than' to add or take away numbers. Remember to use the + and – symbols only if children have been introduced to formal recording.

■ Extending the range of numbers once the children are confident at counting and moving up and down a 0–10 hopscotch grid. For example:

○ 11–20

○ 31–40

○ 100, 200, 300 up to 1,000

■ Encouraging the children to use their own numbers. If you only have ten spaces, which are the best ten numbers to have in your hopscotch grid? Ask them to think about the layout and order of the chosen numbers.

Idea **3.21** Hide-and-seek and other traditional counting games

Recall the games you know from your own childhood which involve counting numbers. Invite parents and grandparents to share their childhood games too. By counting aloud it is easy to see who is counting in order. A game such as hide-and-seek can be extended by challenging children to:

■ Count beyond ten.

■ Start with a number of their choosing to begin and end counting.

■ Count backwards.

Idea **3.22** Number hunts beyond the outdoor space

When out and about, challenge the children to find the biggest number they can. Decide how to keep a record: will the children take photos of the numbers, write them down or record their findings in other ways?

Search for interesting numbers in unexpected places. What makes a number interesting? What places or objects have numbers which have surprised the children?

Is it possible to collect numbers in order as a group? Start by looking for zero, then one, two, three and so on. Photograph and date each number as it is found. The

children may be able to help out with this activity at home – in this way, the project can last all year. A similar activity can be undertaken with numbers of objects: one litter bin, two park benches, three beech trees and so on.

Idea 3.23 Environmental numbers

Environmental numbers provide children with examples of the purpose of numbers. Look for obvious signs and symbols such as:

- Traffic signs: consider the purpose of the shape as well as the numbers and what these represent.

- Lamp posts: each one has a number. Can the children find and read the numbers? Discuss why each lamp post would need a number. Find out at which end of the street they start.

- Shop window displays: what numbers are present and why? Discuss terms such as 'sale' and 'bargain'.

- Fire hydrants: an 'H' sign shows the location of the hydrant below the ground, where it is connected to the water mains. Each one has a number. They should also display the pipe diameter, distance from the access point and a barcode.

- Information labels: playground equipment, benches and other outdoor features often have a label tucked away with all sorts of information on it such as date of manufacture.

- Numbers on doors: look for a pattern. Can the children see that odd numbers are on one side of a street and even numbers are on the other? This is a good reason to walk on both sides of a street.

- Bus numbers and car number plates: where does each bus go? How can we find out? What car number plates catch the children's attention and why? Look at the use of numbers to represent letters.

- Hidden nature numbers: in nature, numbers are often hidden within the structure of an object or feature. Look for numbers in the natural environment. For example:

  ○ 0 – a hole in a tree trunk or the cross-section of a tree

  ○ 1 – a blade of grass

  ○ 2 – the shape made by a swan

Idea 3.24 | Hiding and finding numbers

Many children love hiding and finding games, so this naturally fits with learning to recognise numerals. One option is to conceal numbers in interesting places for the children to stumble upon when playing, such as under a log, mixed in with bark chips or tucked into a stone wall. Stone pebbles, wood cookies and other natural materials work well for this as they can be left outside and will survive several months of weathering.

- Children like to hide numbers in soil or sand. When this happens, encourage them to spin around a couple of times and then see if they can work out where they have hidden their numbers. If it is three-dimensional, can they work out by feeling it which number it is, before pulling it out and checking?

- In a woodland, children enjoy dropping numbers into rotten tree stumps and pulling them out again. Remember to check that no animal is hiding inside beforehand.

- Have bath time foam numbers floating in the water area. Also include numbers on stone pebbles which sink.

- Have flowerpots and buckets which can be used for peekaboo games in which the children take turns to guess which number might be under a flowerpot.

The amount of challenge depends on the age and development of the children. For some, just the experience of feeling, moving and talking about numbers is sufficient. If you have put out different sorts of numbers, such as floating and sinking ones, the children may want to match them to each other, or order and count the numbers.

Idea 3.25 Games around collecting numbers

For example, the children may want to:

- Pick a number and find a number of objects that matches this (e.g. eight dandelions).

- Play hunt the thimble but with specific numbers of objects. For instance, show the children the number five and a picture of five items which have been hidden around the outdoor space (e.g. dinosaurs). If the children have a particular interest (e.g. Lego men), then set up the outdoor space so they have to search for these objects. This can help them to explore and get to know their outdoor space.

- Hide numbers which are then ordered as they are found (see Idea 3.24).

Idea 3.26 Making a staircase number line

When the children have found and brought interesting objects to a gathering circle, then a simple pictorial representation of a number line can be created. As the photo indicates, it is a good way of demonstrating the relationship between the number and the quantity represented, as well as pictorially representing the position of different numbers in relation to each other:

Think about when and where this method of sorting and displaying objects would be appropriate. Why not make a staircase number line on some steps?

Idea 3.27 The number sorting factory

Set up a place for putting any found numbers and objects. This could be in a circle of wooden stumps, a builder's tray, number den, special tree or another place outside. The children can bring numbers or objects here to sort, organise and display them in different ways. It can be helpful to brainstorm possibilities with the children and to get them to help create the area. For example, you might put out cans or bamboo pots with numbers on them. The found objects are added to each pot.

Other useful additions to the area may include:

- Trays, baskets or arrays for sorting. Egg boxes come in different shapes and sizes and are useful for this purpose.
- A mini washing line for pegging up numbers in order. Write numbers on objects and get the children to peg them up in number order or write numbers on the pegs.
- A blank 10 x 10 grid for laying out numbers of objects to make patterns and connections.
- Giant counting lines. You can thread pieces of wood or wicker balls onto a rope. The children can move them along as they count. These can also be numbered.

Idea 3.28 Rope line hoops

Hang numbered hoops or bike tyres from a rope line at a height low enough for the children to step through. They can enjoy climbing through the hoops and can be challenged to do so in the correct order. Mix up the order or make it completely random to extend this activity.

The hoops can be given different numbers. For example:

- Start at 3 and go up to 13.
- Tens: 10, 20, 30, etc.
- Hundreds: 100, 200, 300, etc.
- Selection of numbers (e.g. 1, 2, 5, 9, 12).
- Different sorts of numbers (e.g. a mix of mirrored and laminated number tiles).

┌ ─ ─ ─ ─ ─ ─ ─ ─ ─ ┐
¦ Idea **3.29** ¦ Encountering
└ ─ ─ ─ ─ ─ ─ ─ ─ ─ ┘ negative
                      numbers

Negative numbers can be informally introduced when the need arises in a real context.
For instance, temperature charts and water
depth metres both use scales which include
negative numbers. Other examples include:

- Basement floors in blocks of flats go
  below ground level.

- The depth of a hole can be measured as
  a negative number.

- Sunken gardens help children to feel
  and experience being below ground
  level.

- Experiencing shallow bodies of water
  that go below surface level: stepping
  into puddles, ponds and gently flowing
  streams. Use a measuring stick to gauge
  the depth.

┌ ─ ─ ─ ─ ─ ─ ─ ─ ─ ┐
¦ Idea **3.30** ¦ Zero
└ ─ ─ ─ ─ ─ ─ ─ ─ ─ ┘

Zero is a fascinating symbol. Children have
to learn about the abstract and concrete uses
of zero.

Firstly, it can represent nothing or none.
When objects in a set are removed, eventually you are left with zero or no objects. This
can be practised easily through routines and
activities where items are shared out until
there are no more left or by removing items

from a set until there are zero items left, or it can happen through singing songs such as 'Ten Green Bottles'.

Secondly, on a number line or scale, where it is a whole number like any other, it represents a position. Giving children opportunities to experience negative numbers as outlined in Idea 3.29 can help them to learn about the positional value of zero.

Finally, zero is a placeholder and this concept is developed through work on place value – for example, in the number 203, the zero prevents the number being read as 23. For most children, learning about zero as a placeholder comes later on in their school life.

Idea 3.31 Thinking about big numbers

Children are fascinated with big numbers. The concept of one million is interesting and listening to children count can give an indication of their understanding of the number system. For example, one four-year-old told me he could count to 'one-million-and-ninety-nine'. He counted perfectly to one-hundred-and-ninety-nine at which point he moved on to one thousand. When he reached one-thousand-and-ninety-nine, his next number was one million.

Children enjoy discovering big numbers, trying to read them and also making up their own. If children are talking about numbers such as 'thirty-twelve' then ask them to write it down or offer to scribe. The excitement of this is discovering the possibility that an even bigger number exists such as '3012'. Bear in mind, too, the colloquial use of numbers within our language. Quite often dates are expressed as 'twenty-sixteen' for '2016'.

Idea 3.32 | Infinity

If children are interested in the concept of infinity, you need to ensure you emphasise that it is not a real number. It is not a quantity and it is not countable. It is about the endlessness of our number system or the boundlessness of something. Sadly, this means that Buzz Lightyear will never go 'to infinity and beyond' from a mathematical perspective.

Although mathematicians have assigned it a symbol and are able to explain what infinity is mathematically, in the real world it is much harder to illustrate. The discussion becomes more philosophical and linked to ideas such as 'forever'. Some starting points include:

■ Looking up at a blue sky in the day or a clear sky at night and knowing that you are staring into space. Does space go on forever? Is it infinite?

■ Positioning two mirrors opposite each other so that you see the reflection in each mirror going on forever.

■ Respectful discussions about death when this is encountered (e.g. upon finding a dead animal or mini-beast).

CHAPTER 4

Number Functions and Fractions

In Chapter 3 we considered the need for children to be able to count, sort, order, match and recognise numbers. The concepts of cardinality and ordinality were introduced. Once children have developed their understanding of number, the processes of addition, subtraction, multiplication and division build upon these early concepts, further enabling them to extend their mathematical skills and reasoning.

In their daily lives, young children will be exposed to situations in routines and in their play where there is a need to add, subtract, multiply or divide. For example:

- A child joins the gathering circle at the end of the day and everyone moves up to make one more space.

- A parent arrives to collect their child, leaving one fewer in the group.

- An apple is cut up and shared equally amongst a group of four children.

- Bulbs are planted in clumps of threes to make their layout more attractive.

As educators, we can gently draw children's attention to these events in ways which make a clear link to the maths involved.

Addition

There are two aspects to addition that children need to grasp. The first is the combining of two or more sets into one set – for example, two circles of children may join together to make one larger circle.

The second type is counting on from a known number. This is easily illustrated on a number line. For instance, you may have your finger touching number five and then you count on three more, or you may have five objects and count on three more.

Some children feel secure with the first type of addition. However, it is a conceptual jump for many to keep a number in their head whilst counting on. Think how many times a child will repeatedly count the digits on one hand, even though they may know they have five digits. It is an important part of developing confidence and understanding the 'five-ness of five' – the cardinal aspect of number. This conceptual leap can be repeatedly modelled in different ways. For example, if children are collecting pine cones, they can put five cones in one bag. When three more are found, they can count on three more and then check by counting the total. This then enables the progression to counting on and number line counting.

Vocabulary

A further amount, a little, a lot, add, add together, altogether, another one, array, bigger, count back, count on, divide, double, fraction, equal, grown by, half, half an hour, half past, halve, how many, how much now, increased, left over, less than, many, minus, more than, multiply, number, one, one more, one less, pair, part of, pieces, quarter, quarter past, quarter to, remove, semi-circle, separate, share equally, split, subtract, sum, take away, third, three-quarters, thrice, total, trio, triple, twice, two-thirds, whole, zero

Expressions

In addition to

It all adds up

A problem shared is a problem halved

One bitten, twice shy

Halfway

Half full and half empty

A fraction of a time

Idea 4.1 | When should I introduce the symbols +, −, = ?

It is worth bearing in mind the research cited in Chapter 2 regarding mark making and symbolism. There is a risk that children's confidence and creativity is hampered if we introduce and insist that they use mathematical symbols when they are very young or not developmentally ready. Recognition of the symbols comes before the conceptual understanding. Saying that, there are many commercially available games which use the operational symbols, and children can be made aware of these without the expectation that they use them in their own mark making.

Idea 4.2 Partitioning numbers

Children are naturally interested in partitioning long before this is formally connected to number operations. There are many opportunities for partitioning numbers and developing an understanding of addition and subtraction. It is about breaking groups into sub-groups. Look for opportunities to comment on this when it happens. For example:

- Part of a group may be on one side of a stream and the rest are on the other side.

- Several children are up a tree and the others are on the ground.

- Two rabbits live in one cage and a guinea pig in another, making three animals altogether.

- Several birds are at a feeder and one flies away.

Remember to highlight the numbers in each sub-group and the total. For instance, when putting items into a backpack to go for a walk or an off-site visit, you can ask for the children's advice: 'I have a problem. I have these five items which need to go into my rucksack. I'm wondering which should go into the top compartment and which are better in the main compartment. What do you think?' From here, you can have a discussion and the children can try packing up the rucksack in different ways. Intuitively, they will be considering the size and shape of both the objects and the rucksack when deciding on the number of things to put in each compartment.

When playing circle games with a small group, always count the number of children in the circle. Highlight the partitioning as part of the conversation within the game – for example, 'We need one person in the middle and nine of us to stay around the outside of the circle.'

Idea 4.3 Target practice and other scoring games

Any games involving counting, recording, adding up or taking away are popular. Targets can be drawn or created on walls as well as on the ground. These can be traditional bullseye targets, a single hoop or a series of separate targets.

- Snow can be flattened and painted with food colouring, or simply draw into soft snow with a heel.

- Beaches provide multiple opportunities for raised targets as well as flat ones. Children like building a mound of sand to climb up and then using this to drop shells and stones from a height onto a target (make sure no one is sunbathing below!).

- Sticks are good for making temporary outlines in places where chalk should not be used.

- Woodland litter can be removed to reveal the bare earth (remember to scatter the litter back over when you've finished). How many pine cones land in the circle compared to those that don't?

- Place hoops on the ground or hang them up. Just add beanbags! How many bags make it into the hoop and how many fall outside the hoop?

- Skittles games work on the same principle. How many get knocked over? How many are still standing? You can replace the skittles with cans or bottles (see Idea 3.13).

Idea 4.4 Using a pair of dice

Introduce games in which a pair of dice are needed. This automatically means the children are learning how to add. The addition process occurs in several ways:

- Children count the dots on one dice and then continue counting the dots on the second dice.

- Children recognise the layout of dots on one dice and then count on: 'That's five plus three. Let's count – five, six, seven, eight.'

- Children recognise the layout of dots on both dice and add up mentally without needing to count any dots.

Remember that dots need to come before numerals when using dice. Do not introduce numbered dice until lots of practice has been had counting and recognising the dot patterns. When numbered dice are introduced, it is possible to purchase or make ones with only 1, 2 and 3 marked on them. You can apply the same technique to subtracting numbers on the dice.

> When we are walking out and about, we take a big pair of dice. One has the digits, the other the dot patterns. I throw the dice over my shoulder. A child will pick them up and add the numbers and the dots together. They quickly associate the digits with the dot pattern. They also like to throw the dice over their shoulders! My dot dice are indented. This enables the younger children to put stones into the dots and match the quantity to the dot pattern.
>
> Unnur Henrys, pre-school teacher, Iceland

Idea 4.5 | Under the flowerpot

Take a flowerpot and find some objects that will fit underneath. For very young children, three objects will be enough.

Count the number of objects with the children first. Next, ask them to close their eyes whilst you hide some of the objects underneath the flowerpot. Get the children to open their eyes and predict how many objects are under the flowerpot. Then have a conversation and explore how many are still present before revealing the hidden objects. Repeat the game but let each child have a go at hiding some objects.

The game can be made easier by using a cloth to hide hard objects, such as stones, underneath. The children can check their answer by feeling the stones before responding. Another version of the game is to hide fingers and thumbs if children have the dexterity to do so.

Idea 4.6 | Stick tapping and listening games

Games which build upon the stick tapping suggestions in Idea 3.19 provide encounters with a different form of addition and subtraction. For example, if the children are learning their number bonds to ten, one child can tap a number and the rest of the group have to tap back the complementary number to make ten.

Idea 4.7 'Show me' games

This is a small group activity which works best in a place with lots of objects, such as a pile of leaves or a mound of gravel. The adult makes statements such as:

- Show me three pieces of gravel.
- Now show me more than three pieces of gravel.
- Add one more.
- Now take two pieces away.

Once the children get the idea, they can take it in turns to call out instructions for the rest of the group to follow. It is a useful way of assessing their understanding of language. It can sometimes help to get the children to lay out their objects in a line or as an array.

Idea 4.8 Add or subtract?

This is a variation of Idea 4.7. Each child begins with five objects. The adult has two bags. One contains two cards – one says 'add' and the other 'subtract'. In the other bag are three pebbles with the numbers zero, one and two painted on them – use the dot layout of dice to begin with.

The adult pulls out one card and one of the number pebbles. The children have to add or subtract the quantity shown from their five objects. The game ends when a child has no objects left. Once the children have got the hang of the game they can change the rules or take turns to pull the pebbles out of the bag. By changing the cards you can introduce or reinforce key vocabulary.

Idea 4.9 How many ways?

Each pair of children has two baskets and five natural objects (e.g. stones). The children have to decide how many different ways there are of dividing the stones between the baskets (e.g. three stones in one basket, two stones in the other). These can be recorded as the child sees fit. This works best as part of a narrative story made up with the children.

Idea 4.10 Pavement pick-a-number

Two children each choose a number between zero and ten. Starting on the same pavement slab, they count aloud until they reach their number and step along the corresponding number of paving slabs. The child who picked the smallest number then has to work out how many more steps they need to take to reach the other child.

Idea 4.11 Adding on games

Adding on games are useful for learning the concept of addition. The children in the group need a pile of objects such as pine cones or stones. They collectively agree a number, such as twelve. The children take it in turns to put one or two objects into the centre of the circle. As they do so, the group needs to keep count of how many are in the centre. The aim of the game is not to be the person who puts the twelfth object into the centre – that child loses and everyone else wins. The loser can choose the next number to reach.

Subtraction

Children need distinct experiences to help them develop their understanding of subtraction. It is an umbrella term which covers a variety of structures.

Partitioning

The most straightforward subtraction scenario is that of taking away or removing part of a set to create a subset. Imagine your children find ten apples underneath a tree. The apples may be sorted into those that are suitable for eating and those that aren't. The edible ones are removed and the inedible ones are left.

Using arrays and fixed layouts can help children to see the number of objects being removed. If a child collects six pine cones in an egg box and gives two of them to a friend, it is easy to see the missing two cones and to count that four are left in the box. Tens frames are useful for this purpose.

Counting back

The counting back form of subtraction is a little more complex and is the ordinal aspect of subtraction. A child has to know the sequence of numbers backwards as well as forwards, and remember how many have been taken away as well as how many are left. Try the following outside:

- Using fingers to count back.

- Using paving slabs and other environmental number lines to count back (see Idea 3.17).

- Using objects such as number pebbles which can be flipped over when counted.

- Using a pocket number line (see Idea 3.18).

- Singing number songs and rhymes which focus on this aspect of subtraction (see Idea 2.3).

Comparing quantities and finding the difference

Lots of practical work is needed to demonstrate this type of subtraction. If the edible apples are put in one line and the inedible ones in another line alongside, then it is easier for direct visual comparisons to occur and for the children to see which line has more apples and which has fewer. Questions such as, 'How many more/fewer …?' can be asked as well as, 'I wonder what the difference is between the number of edible and inedible apples?'

When the numerical difference is stated, it helps to articulate using different statements so the children learn that each statement represents the equivalent situation. For example, 'There are seven edible apples and three rotten apples. There are four more edible apples than rotten ones. There are three fewer rotten apples than edible ones.' The final stage is comparisons with the total such as:

- Ten is seven more than three.

- Ten is three more than seven.

- Seven must be added to three to make ten.

- Three must be added to seven to make ten.

Idea 4.12 : The game of nim

With a partner, the children collect twenty stones, pine cones or other small objects to use as counters. Taking it in turns, each child chooses to pick up one, two or three counters. The player who picks up the last counter loses the game. Once the children understand the gist of the game they can change it to suit themselves. For example, they may decide to have fifteen pebbles and take away up to four in any one go.

An alternative is to start with one pebble and then add one, two or three pebbles to see if it is possible to make ten. As the children's addition skills grow, the game can be extended to adding up to fifteen or twenty. This is particularly useful as a game that teaches children to add by counting on, with the adult modelling this practice.

Multiplication

Multiplication comes in two guises:

1 The repeated addition of sets of equal objects – for example, there may be ten pairs of wellies sitting on a welly rack.

2 Scaling – this is about making something so many times bigger or heavier (e.g. twice as large, three times heavier). Scaling is also about making objects smaller or lighter. It begins with doubling or halving quantities.

Children need opportunities to explore the commutative aspect of multiplication – that is, the order in which the sets are counted makes no difference to the total, so there are four different ways of counting six objects. Rectangular arrays are helpful for commutative aspect and partitioning activities, demonstrating that 6 x 1, 1 x 6, 2 x 3 and 3 x 2 are all different ways of laying out and counting six objects.

Once a child has mastered counting forwards and backwards, then they are ready to experience counting in groups of numbers. Counting in twos, fives or tens would be the absolute most you would expect of children at this stage for counting on in steps. Possibilities include:

- Climbing steps two at a time and counting in twos as this happens.
- Jumping and landing on every other paving slab when out for a walk.
- Counting bundles of ten sticks in tens.
- Laying out sticks in groups of five as the beginning of tallying.
- Using arrays for sorting, counting and holding objects.

Idea 4.13 Nature multiplication

It can be fun to build up a photo collection of multiplication examples from outside. These can be added to a big book along with examples of pressed and dried plants. Illustrations of multiplication can be found in humans, animals and plants:

- Humans have two legs. When three humans go for a walk, count and discover that six legs are used.

- Cats have four legs. When you see two cats, you can count eight legs.

- If you pick ten three-leaved clover plants, you will have thirty leaves.

Idea 4.14 Exploring arrays

A 10 x 10 grid is useful for exploring arrays as it can help children to decide on the arrays they will create. Invent challenges based upon what children find outside. For example:

- How many different rectangular arrays can you make with twelve pine cones?

- What is similar about these patterns?

- If you only have five pine cones, what patterns are possible in a 3 x 3 grid?

Idea 4.15 Circle jump

In this party game, the children have to dance around circles placed or drawn on the ground. When the adult calls out a number (e.g. two) everyone has to jump into a circle, but only two children are allowed in each one. The next time call out 'three', then 'four'. The children can estimate the number of circles needed for each number called out. Discuss how many circles are needed each time and how many children are left over. The activity can be varied by asking the children to work out other quantities, such as the number of noses in a circle or the number of elbows.

Idea 4.16 Multiplication scavenger hunt

This gathering approach to introducing multiplication can be used to illustrate the concept of doubling when two children with equal amounts of objects put their separate piles together. Each group picks an object (e.g. cones) and a number (e.g. six). If two children are in the group, then each child must create a pile of six cones. Two piles of six cones equals twelve cones altogether. Once one challenge is finished, the group may choose a different number and a different object to collect. Encourage the children to consider how they will record their work. Assemble a range of objects in advance such as sticks, a particular species of cone or stones.

Division

Division can be embedded into practice in practical ways. As with multiplication, the language of division should be modelled by staff whenever possible. Even if the calculations are too difficult, talk aloud as you solve them. There are several ways of thinking about division which include:

- Division is about the equal sharing of quantity, weight or another form. It involves breaking up a set into a number of equal groups.

- Division is the inverse of multiplication. For example, fifteen flowers can be put into three groups of five flowers or five groups of three flowers. This is where using arrays and encouraging children to consider how they are splitting sets of objects matters.

- Division is also repeated subtraction of equal amounts. If there are fifteen flowers, then how many times can we take away three flowers from the fifteen until there are none left? This aspect benefits from the use of a number line to explain. This is also related to the grouping model of division (e.g. 'We have twelve cones, how many groups of two can we make?').

From a mathematical perspective, care needs to be taken when using the word 'share' for experiences of sharing that do not correspond to division, such as sharing in the social sense of the word.

Sharing involves breaking up a set into a number of equal groups. This is mostly undertaken by children in tasks where resources are being shared. For example:

- Gardening equipment such as trowels may need to be shared equally along with pots when potting up seeds or bulbs.

- Storing equipment: provide containers and baskets which have integral dividers for dividing, sorting and organising resources. Alternatively, add in simple dividers made from scrap wood or cardboard.

- The sharing of counters at the start of a game.

Fractions

A fraction is often described as something that is part of a whole. By sharing a set of items equally in a group and splitting whole objects into smaller parts, the children are introduced to practical examples of fractions. Rather than jump straight away into number work, spend time using shapes and objects to embed the concept of what one-half, one-quarter and one-third mean.

The language and vocabulary around fractions requires careful thought to avoid giving children confusing messages. For example, when cutting an apple in half, it can be more helpful to emphasise that the resulting halves are two parts of *one* apple rather than part of a *whole* apple. When referring to a mixed fraction such as 1¼, we say 'One and a quarter' not 'A whole and a quarter'.

When we break an object roughly into fractions we are measuring in a way that is imprecise and approximate. When we are counting (e.g. half of eight counters) we can be mathematically precise. This is a subtle point but one we need to be mindful of in preparation for children's understanding of measurement. Thus, when objects are split, if the resulting parts are unequal then they cannot be a half, a quarter and so on. It is important to avoid phrases like 'You can have the biggest half.' This is mathematically inaccurate.

When the fractions or equal parts of an object are put back together, they should make one object. Let children have time to try putting two halves or four quarters back together.

Thus, there is a precision to fractions which we need to be mindful of, even when working outside with natural objects.

Idea 4.17 Drawing children's attention to objects and their separate parts

This can be achieved through examining different parts of a whole: realising that one plant has roots, flowers, a stem and petals or that a house has a roof, windows, doors and walls.

Idea 4.18 Breaking objects

To begin with, young children need lots of experiences to split, rip, tear, cut and fold objects into smaller equal parts. Many children enjoy the physical act of removing or taking away a part. For example:

- Construction kits which involve building then deconstructing or breaking up the assembly into separate parts.

- Breaking things like sticks apart or tearing leaves and then trying to fit them back together, or pulling a cap off a mushroom stem and trying to put it back on.

- A tinkering area where larger items can be taken apart, such as an old bicycle.

- Undoing constructions created as part of junk modelling.

Idea 4.19 The perfect half

An impromptu challenge is to break a dead twig or thin stick into two equal parts that are exactly the same length. It is quite tricky and the halves that are created need to be treasured. Naturally, the challenge can then move on to creating quarters and thirds.

A similar challenge can happen when on a leaf hunt. Is it possible to find a leaf that will fold perfectly down the midrib? Is it possible to tear a leaf into two halves? This can be further extended through the leaf fractions counting challenge (see Idea 4.22).

From these beginnings, further work can emerge involving groups of objects being shared equally.

Idea 4.20 Fraction decision-making

Take a twig and break it in two to help make decisions: whoever gets the longest part makes the final decision. If the twig is broken precisely in half then two people get to agree the decision. It's a variation of the short straw.

Idea 4.21 Fractions in the outdoor space

There are many possibilities for sharing out resources between children, splitting whole objects into smaller parts or where halves, quarters and thirds can be illustrated as the children play. When sharing objects, introduce the language of fractions. Try some of the following:

- Provide cutters and slicers for flattening and dividing up soft materials such as mud, sand or snow. An old cake slice is also useful.

- Draw lines around containers which accurately mark the halfway point. This can be linked to exploring capacity using clear crystal tubes or one litre tubs (fill with 500 ml of water to find the exact level). Alternatively, tape the 50 cm mark on one metre sticks.

- Add silver duct tape to tarps to identify half or a quarter of the sheet. This can be useful for informal play as well as for ensuring there is enough space for the children to sit.

- Offer a mix of containers of known capacities, such as one litre and 500 ml ice cream containers or measuring cups of one cup and half-a-cup sizes.

Idea 4.22 Leaf fractions counting challenge

Understanding the sequencing of fractions is valuable and leaf fractions can help. Ask every child to find a leaf. This works best if the leaves are all the same species and have approximately the same surface area (e.g. beech leaves). Next, request that each leaf is split into two parts. The children take it in turns to place their leaf on a line starting with half of one leaf, then two halves of one leaf, two halves of one leaf plus half of another leaf and so on. As each half leaf is placed the group can count: half, one, one-and-a-half, two, two-and-a-half, three and so on.

A display of materials to help with counting simple fractions can be created from this and similar activities. Some plants have leaf or petal arrangements which are made for sharing equally.

Idea 4.23 Half art

Lots of artwork can be undertaken with halves of leaves and other gathered materials which can be accurately halved. For young children, simply creating half a picture can be sufficient – perhaps another child can use the other half of the sheet or area to create their half picture. More able children may be interested in creating symmetrical pictures where the line of symmetry splits the work in half.

Idea 4.24 Simple sharing and scoring games

The links between division and the equal sharing of objects and fractions can be introduced. For example, if a child is sharing a pile of objects, such as collected shells, with a friend then suggest this is done by drawing a circle in the sand with a line to show two halves. The children share the shells between the two halves of the circle. Is each side equal? How many are in each side? We have shared them into two equal groups so half the shells are in each group: how many are there in each group? This half of the number we started with.

There are many opportunities for playing simple games which further develop an understanding of fractions through objects. Simple throwing games, such as aiming for a circle on the ground with a set of five cones, is a good example. How many cones make it into the circle and how many are outside? Point out that two out of five cones are outside and three out of five cones are inside, and then highlight that we can say this as a fraction – three-fifths.

CHAPTER 5

Money

Children need to be able to recognise a range of coins and develop an awareness of how money is used. The opportunities for some children to gain practical experience of handling money are increasingly limited as more families use cards for transactions and bank or shop online. Thus, creating situations for children to be exposed to money in their play and everyday routines matters. Learning how to handle money is the beginning of financial literacy.

Some children, because of their background or culture, develop their understanding of money from an early age. It can be a gateway to other number work and provide a meaningful context for learning other number processes. Coins have fascinating detail and there is a story or reason behind every design. For example, the newer the British coin, the older Queen Elizabeth looks. Provide a range of magnifiers so the children can look at the shape and detail of different coins.

Experiences of money could involve the following:

- Free play which allows the children to play with money outside as well as in.
- Routines that include the use of money (e.g. Ideas 12.18, 12.19).
- Traditional, multicultural and invented money games.
- Folklore and the natural world, which have links to money and, often, the concept of luck.

It is worth asking parents and carers for their ideas and experiences as there are traditions from different cultures which can be used as learning opportunities. When children visit different countries, request that any spare coins are donated to your class. The children can compare these to British coins. For children who have family in other countries, developing an understanding of their monetary system could be of practical value if they visit regularly.

Family support for using money can also be helpful. For example, parents can:

- Allow children to pay for public transport.
- Provide a little pocket money that is issued in small change.
- Encourage children to check prices and count out money when shopping with small amounts of cash.
- Play simple money games.
- Ask the tooth fairy to provide small change.
- Encourage children to regularly check the back of a sofa and under seats for loose change.
- Provide a piggy bank so the children can add coins and also check to see the total that has been saved.

One difficulty that children face is understanding the monetary system. Where coins do not exist for a specific number, such as three pence, it requires a higher level of reasoning to understand that this amount can be created through offering three pennies or one two pence coin and one penny coin. Lots of practice at matching and exchanging coins is needed using small amounts.

Money also can help children begin to understand the concept of associated numbers. This is especially difficult since this concept is vague for most children during their early years. A child may value two pennies more than one twenty pence piece because of the perception that more (two) is better than less (one), despite their relative value. Discussions about representational mathematics become crucial when it comes to money.

The practical experience of real life shopping can help children begin to learn the complex relationship between the price of an item, money and value. Prices are subject to change. This can be most clearly seen during a sale. In role play around shops, creating sale prices and offers such as 'Buy one, get one free' enables children to learn experientially about changing costs. This can be linked to traditional sale times throughout the year – for example, January sales. Money is also useful for helping children to understand the concept of zero. When they have spent money and have none left, the concept of zero takes on a new meaning.

Vocabulary

Bargain, change, cheap, cost, discount, euros, expensive, how much, less than, more than, pence, pennies, pounds, price, quid, sale, swap, swipe, value

Expressions

Money doesn't grow on trees

Money can't buy happiness

Look after your pennies and the pounds will take care of themselves

---

Idea 5.1 Flip a coin and penny walks

It can be fun to flip a coin to help make decisions. Let the children do this once they realise how it affects their decision-making. For example, it can be used to decide which person starts a game or is the leader of a group. Each adult can carry a coin in their pocket for this purpose.

Penny walks provide an exciting approach to decision-making. At each junction, flip a coin. If the coin lands heads up, the group takes the road to the right. If the coin lands tails up, the group takes the road to the left. Have a guess where the group will end up. Practitioners do need to know their local area very well in advance of this activity.

Idea 5.2 | Visiting local shops and services

Role play starts with real experiences. Go for a walk down a street with some shops on it. Look in the windows at the goods on sale and the price tags. Ask nicely for takeaway menus to use in role play. Watch how customers pay for an item and what the person at the till does. Use the experience to develop role play back at your setting. Role play can come to life when staff are engaged with the play, modelling the use of money and conversation, and doing it meaningfully.

Idea 5.3 | Using money during free play in your outdoor space

Using real money wherever possible makes the experience more authentic. It helps the children become familiar with the different shape, weight, size, colour and value of each coin. They get opportunities to learn the vocabulary associated with money. There doesn't need to be a lot of coins available, but a sufficient number for the children to be able to use them in their play. For example:

- Provide a few coins in purses.

- Ensure the occasional coin is left lying around in the outdoor space (e.g. hidden in bark chips or balanced on a ledge in a playhouse) to be discovered another day.

- The children may wish to bury and find coins in a sand tray or the digging area.

- Fish for money. One penny coins are magnetic so can be put in buckets of water or hidden around the grounds for children to collect using a fishing rod magnet.

- Create treasure boxes and put coins in them which can be hidden in the outdoor space for others to find and then count the money! Use clues like 'warmer' and 'colder' to find the boxes. The children can take it in turns to hide the box. This works well if the children are playing pirates.

In large nurseries it simply may not be feasible to have lots of real money available, and replenishing supplies could be expensive. Other substitutes can work: as well as plastic coins, a natural approach is to use 'wood pennies' – thin slices of wood. Older children are quite happy to use natural objects to represent money (e.g. stone = 1p, leaf = 2p, pine cone = 5p).

Idea 5.4 Will a spider make you rich?

If children are interested in spiders, then take time to find out about money spiders. Do they bring greater wealth if you see one and let it live?

Idea 5.5 Plop buckets

Stick a ten pence coin to the bottom of a bucket and then fill it up with water. Children enjoy dropping pennies into the bucket and seeing if they can make them land exactly on the ten pence coin. Count how much money has been dropped once the target is hit and begin again. Change the value of the coins as the children's understanding and ability to count improves.

Idea 5.6 Pitch and toss

Pitch and toss is a traditional playground game. A group of children stand behind a line in front of a wall. Each person needs a penny coin. Each child takes a turn to carefully throw their coin against the wall. The winner is the child whose coin lands closest to the wall. That person collects all the money thrown and the next round begins. To increase the level of challenge, use two pence coins, then a mixture of one and two pence coins. Build up the coins used in line with the children's interests and abilities.

Idea 5.7 | Coin throw

Coin throw is a traditional Chinese game, played with real coins. Each child holds a coin up against a wall, making sure the edge of the coin is touching the wall. Then they let it drop. The person whose coin rolls furthest away from the wall begins. The child should pick up their coin but mark its place with their foot. They must not move from this spot. They then carefully throw the coin at the other coins. If the coin touches another coin, the child wins it. If they miss, then everyone picks up their coin and starts again. Any child who has lost a coin to someone else will need another coin to get back into the game.

Idea 5.8 | Real treasure hunts

Old coins can be a source of interest when talking about then and now. Make sure the children have time to examine these and compare the coins to money which is currently in use. Encourage the children to find the dates on coins and learn how to read them.

Old money is often found in the ground. It can be an interesting experiment to bury some money. Get the children to take photos of the money first and then bury it in the ground. The children may wish to create a treasure map so they know the location of the money. After several months, dig it up and compare its condition to when it was buried. Was all the money found?

Idea 5.9 | Make a wish for charity

In some communities you can throw coins into wishing wells to make a wish. Other local attractions may have ponds or similar charity fundraising opportunities. Encourage the children to look out for charity boxes of different sorts both inside and outside shops and other amenities. Talk about their purpose and donate some change if you can.

Idea 5.10 | Holding an outdoor sale as a fundraiser

If your school or setting participates in a village fete, then let the children experience this and set up a similar event in your outdoor space for other children or parents/carers to visit. The children can make and buy little objects such as garden plants, collections of sticks, painted stones and so on. Discuss what is a suitable price to charge and request that the children write the price labels on the goods for sale.

Idea 5.11 Giving children choices over outdoor resources which are bought for the setting

It can be hard for children to understand the cost of different items. Involving children in purchasing decisions can help them begin to appreciate the financial value of a resource.

Cut out photos of different items and stick each of these onto a different jar. Ask the children to vote for which one they would like the setting to purchase. Discuss the idea of a fair vote and letting everyone have their say. You could place a relevant practical or sensory object beside each jar to help the children decide. To provide a visual indication of the cost you could include representative photographs of the money. Remember to talk about each resource, including the pros and cons of each one, so the children make an informed decision.

Once the items have been purchased, put the empty packaging on display to say thank you to parents and others who have made donations. Add photos of the children using the resources and the learning which has arisen as a result.

Idea 5.12 Coin trees and stumps

There is a long-standing tradition of money trees or wishing trees. These tend to be mature trees or aged stumps with coins pushed or hammered into their bark by passers-by who hope it will bring them good fortune. Some are very old with coins buried deep in the bark. Very occasionally ancient beams in houses can be found with coins pushed into their splits. It is believed the tradition dates back to the 1700s. However, there has been a strong resurgence in recent years.

After seeing a coin stump, the children may want to try making one back in the nursery. Brainstorm what could work well – for example, hammering coins into balsa wood is an absorbing challenge.

Idea 5.13 Money trees

Does money grow on trees? This can be a good topic of conversation for children who may wish to see if they can find ways of making a money tree. They might try sticking coins onto trees using clay, or planting coins.

In China, there are legends which have grown up around money trees which are made from glazed earthenware. They are regarded as holy trees which can bring money and fortune to people and are a symbol of wealth. They are popular at Chinese New Year.

A lovely fusion of Scottish and Tibetan cultures has taken place at the Kagyu Samye Ling Buddhist monastery with the creation of a clootie tree.[1] You pay a donation for a piece of scrap material which you tie onto the tree. As you do so, you make a wish or say a prayer of healing for others in your life and in this way money is creatively and positively associated with trees.

---

1 See J. Robertson, The clootie tree, *Creative Star Learning* (19 April 2014). Available at: http://creativestarlearning.co.uk/early-years-outdoors/the-clootie-tree/.

CHAPTER 6

Measurement

Measurement is undertaken to work out the length, size or amount of something. It helps us to carry out many jobs, and yet it relies upon bringing together many basic maths skills such as being able to estimate, count, compare and order numbers, round up and down, scale, add and subtract time intervals and so on. It helps us to quantify and make sense of the world. It is an essential life skill.

If you reflect on your day, it is highly likely you will have measured something. Perhaps it was:

- Checking you have the correct quantities of ingredients to cook a meal.

- Estimating the amount of cereal you will eat or how much butter to put on your toast.

- Holding up a pair of old trousers and wondering if you will still fit them based upon your current weight and clothing size.

This chapter explores size (length, height, depth and width), weight, volume and capacity. This has connections with other areas of maths such as spatial concepts – that is, near and far and the amount of space an object takes up. There are other forms of measurement too, such as area, density and temperature, which can be referred to as and when necessary.

Regardless of the type of measurement being undertaken, there are key concepts and skills which need to be developed:

- Acquiring and understanding vocabulary and expressions relating to measurement. Very young children begin with learning and comparing opposites: big and small, empty and full, heavy and light, long and short, wide and narrow, high and low, fast and slow and so on. This can develop into the use of superlatives.

- Comparing objects and measurements. This starts with the opposites, such as heavy and light, but moves on to understanding and ordering objects according to length, height, weight and so on. Children need experiences in comparing – themselves to each other and to their environment – and to be able to order their comparisons.

- Making sensible estimates. We use our knowledge of measurement to make realistic estimates about how long it will take to do a task or whether an object is too heavy to pick up.

- Understanding conservation of measures. Young children can struggle with the concept of a standardised unit having different appearances. For example:

  o One litre containers come in a variety of shapes but all have the same capacity.

- ○ A big object like a cardboard box may feel lighter compared to a smaller stump of wood.

- ○ When you roll up a thin piece of rope it is the same length as when it is unravelled.

- ○ A piece of clay has the same mass regardless of whether it is rolled out or in a ball.

- ■ Measuring accurately using a range of equipment and objects. Eventually children can read numerical scales relevant to the measurements they undertake.

Idea 6.1 Using non-standard units with young children

Children need lots of different measurement experiences in their play, which begin with non-standard units and include familiar items such as body parts, natural materials and household items. Every item will be a slightly different size or weight which is why they are considered non-standard. There are several reasons for focusing on non-standard units.

Firstly, almost any object known to the children can be used. It is easier to build this form of measuring into children's play, and a child is not having to learn the act of measuring with unfamiliar materials. Mathematical schemata are built upon known experiences. Whether you measure with a tape measure or a found stick is neither here nor there in terms of many of the processes involved.

Outside, adults often use non-standard measurements. Bushcraft work involves using body parts as a measuring tool – for example, making a bow drill for starting a fire involves finding and cutting a curved branch which is the length of your outstretched arm to your chest bone. Children like being able to use their body parts as a measuring tool. It makes direct and personal sense. After all, the first tools used for counting are our fingers.

Another reason for using non-standard materials is that many standardised units of measurement are simply too small or too big for little children. To measure the height of a friend in metres would not make sense to a child because the unit of a metre is too big and because part of a metre has to be used. A measurement such as 1.10 metres has no meaning to a young child. Likewise, trying to count 110 cm is a lot of counting!

Finally, using non-standard units and observing the variation in the results helps children to see the need for a standard unit of measurement. It improves the accuracy of our work. Initially the variation in results provides a springboard into lots of mathematical conversations, reasoning and problem-solving. Eventually, a standard unit becomes more convenient and allows for more precise comparative work.

As well as everyday objects and natural materials, children need experience of using a range of measuring devices such as tape measures, measuring jugs and spoons, metre sticks, coins, stopwatches, timers and so on. They need to be able to measure accurately using these tools.

Idea 6.2 The role of the adult

As with all aspects of maths, adults need to model the appropriate language and take the time to explain what different words and expressions mean. As a staff team, you may find it helpful to discuss and decide on strategies to help everyone remember the accurate terminology and the concepts or meaning behind each word, in particular mass and weight, volume and capacity, and imperial and metric measuring systems.

In addition, adults can:

- Help to model and reinforce the need for accuracy when measuring. This takes time and practice. Children also need to begin to understand that no measurement can ever be 100% accurate – there is always a degree of rounding up or down. The equipment used also affects the accuracy of each measurement.

- Support children in their estimations. Very young children may not always be able to make sensible estimates so scaffolding their responses may help. This means an adult offers two or three possible responses and the child chooses from these.

- Think about the presentation of the measuring tools and layout of resources. They need to be carefully displayed and accessible to the children so they can compare the sizes, shapes and weights of different objects. A jumbled collection of objects in a storage box may affect the choices children make compared to having them hung up or laid out near to where they are used most. Take care to listen to what children suggest and consider this in light of their knowledge and understanding. For example, a child may look at a handful of stones and give the response, 'hundreds'. Rather than assuming the child has made a wild guess, it is quite likely the child telling you that there are lots of stones, possibly more than they are ready to count!

Volume and capacity

Volume is the amount of three-dimensional space an object or substance occupies. Normally volume is measured in cubic centimetres (cm²) or cubic metres (m²). Volume is used to describe the amount of liquid in a container.

Capacity is the size of a container and the volume of liquid it will hold. It is measured in millilitres (ml) and litres (l). 1 litre = 1,000 ml.

In the UK, imperial measurements of capacity are also used and can be seen on many food labels. Petrol used to be sold in gallons and milk in pints. One gallon is the equivalent of eight pints. A pint is just over half a litre. Liquid is measured in fluid ounces (fl. oz.).

Whilst volume and capacity work is often associated with water and sand play outdoors, it also comes into activities such as packing solid objects into containers, for example trolleys or boxes, or judging whether a box has the capacity to hide a child. Filling and pouring is a developmental play activity that children enjoy, so provide lots of opportunities to do this in many different contexts and places.

Vocabulary

Capacity, containers, cubic centimetres, cubic metres, empty, fill, fit, full, half a pint, half-empty, half-full, level, litres, loose, millilitres, overflowing, packed, pint, pour, scoop, size, space, tight, volume

Expressions

Pint sized

Volume of work

Idea 6.3 The biggest splat

If children like pouring water everywhere, then explore volume by looking at which container creates the biggest splat when tipped upside down. Children rather like looking at and talking about splat marks. Water can also be thrown against a wall or poured down a guttering pipe. Use a piece of string or rope to help compare sizes.

A variation of this game is for the children to pour the water over each other (remember to ensure they are appropriately dressed for this one!). Do the children prefer the feeling of being drenched by a large bucket or the trickle of a tiny cupful of water?

Idea 6.4 The longest squirt

Syringes are superb tools for investigating volume through play. The children may need to be shown how to draw water into a syringe. At this point you can draw attention to the scale on the side of each one. Be aware that different sizes of syringe have different scales.

Does the syringe that has the largest capacity create the squirt that travels the furthest? If so, is it because it can hold the biggest volume of water? If you have a choice of syringes, is it better to have two small syringes or one large one?

Idea 6.5 Displaced water

Measure the volume of water in a bucket or jug. What happens when objects are dropped into the water? Does this affect the volume of water in the bucket? How can your children find out? It is worth using a clear container and marking the level of the water so the children can clearly see the movement of the water as it becomes displaced.

Idea 6.6 Making a splash

Most children I know thoroughly enjoy making a splash. Mathematically, this is about investigating the displacement of water – that is, reducing the capacity within a container or vessel so the same volume of liquid is forced out.

- Is it possible to splash all the water out of a puddle?

- If you have a bucket of water, what object will make the biggest splash when dropped into it? Does the height from which you drop the object make a difference? Does the size of the object make a difference? Is it all about the weight of the dropped object?

Idea 6.7 Bubble play

What is the biggest bubble you can make, and what advice can the children give others about creating the bubble which can hold the largest volume of air? Try blowing a bubble through different sized funnels and seeing if this makes a difference.

Idea **6.8** The capacity of balloons

Balloons are exciting. Before filling a balloon, encourage the children to estimate how much water their balloon will hold. Have jugs or syringes of different sizes so the children can begin to quantify the volume of liquid being held in non-standard units. Does the original size of a balloon affect the volume of water it can hold? How could you and the children find out?

Idea **6.9** The filling station game

Children need experiences that help them to understand the concept of full and empty. When a container is full it cannot hold any more water. When a container is empty there is no water in it.

In this game you need one large container and a cup for each child who wants to play – a maximum of four children is probably best. You also need a bucket of water or large puddle which contains more than enough water to fill the large container.

The children take turns to fill their cup right up to the top and then pour the water from the cup into the large container. The person who causes the container to overflow when their water is added loses the game. The person who went before this wins.

Once a group of children have got the hang of this game, encourage them to change different elements of it. For example:

- Change the capacity of the large container. What happens if it becomes smaller? Talk about the capacity of the containers in terms of the number of cups it takes to fill them.

- Change the capacity of the cups used. What happens if they increase in size?

- The children could choose their own container from a range of options. Which one is easiest to fill up? Does it make a difference as to who wins the game?

- What happens if standardised units are used – for instance, if the big container has a capacity of two litres and the cups each have a capacity of a quarter of a litre?

- Change the number of children who play the game.

- Can the children predict who is likely to win before the game begins?

Idea 6.10 Exploring the concept of one litre and other standardised amounts

Introduce containers which have a one litre capacity. These should be in a range of shapes and types so the children begin to develop the concepts of equivalence and conservation. Children often find it hard to comprehend that a small, wide container can hold as much as a taller, thinner one. They need time to pour water between the containers to investigate conservancy.

Once children have had plenty of experience using a variety of one litre containers in their play, then provide half litre containers. This enables numerical comparisons to happen, such as discovering that two half litre containers hold the same volume of liquid as a one litre container.

You can play simple games such as having four containers of different sizes, one of which is half a litre. Beside these containers, place a one litre container. Can the group guess which container holds half as much water as the one litre container? They can use water to check if their guess is correct. Ask the children how they can tell if a container holds half as much as a larger container. Through the filling and pouring that children like to do, suggest that they work out how many quarter litres fill a one litre or a half litre container.

Idea 6.11 The conservancy game

To demonstrate conservancy of capacity, the filling station game (Idea 6.9) can be adapted. Play two rounds, the first one using a one litre container, changing it in the second round for another one litre container that is a different shape.

Fill up the first one litre container using cups of water. Beforehand, estimate how many cups of water are needed to fill a one litre bottle and the number of cups needed to cause the one litre container to overflow. Using the same cups, replay the game with the second, differently shaped one litre container. What do the children observe?

Idea 6.12 Exploring the musical properties of volume and capacity

Collect several glass jars and get the children to fill them with water to different levels. Then listen to the sounds made when the glasses are tapped with sticks, spoons and other items.

- Does the capacity of the jar affect the sound or is it the volume of the water it contains? Or is it a bit of both? How can you experiment and find out?

- What happens if all your jars have the same capacity and shape – is the sound made affected by the amount of water?

- Will the addition of food colouring change the pitch? What happens if other items are added to the water in the jars?

- Try ordering the jars according to the different quantities of water so the children can hear the changing pitch.

- Remember to talk about 'more than' and 'less than'.

In my experience, most children can be trusted to use glass items sensibly. However, agree some basic rules around their use. Occasionally an item will break, which is part of the learning process. The children should know to avoid using the area until the shards have all been collected and safely disposed of by an adult.

Idea 6.13 Sandcastles

Building sandcastles helps children to learn about volume and capacity. There are tricks to building sandcastles, such as packing down the sand and levelling it off, which are useful skills for measuring purposes. Snow castles are just as much fun to build in the winter months. Experiment with different containers to see which make the best castles.

Weight and mass

Weight is how heavy an object is. It is the pull of gravity acting on the mass of an object. It is a force which is measured in newtons.

Mass is the measure of the quantity of matter. When you hold an object you feel its weight, not its mass. The weight of an object depends upon the gravitational pull from the core of the earth. If we were on a different planet, such as Jupiter, where the gravitational pull is significantly greater, then we would weigh more too. However, our body mass would remain constant. Mass is measured in grams (g) and kilogrammes (kg). 1 kg = 1,000 g.

This can be confusing, so it isn't surprising that many educators decide not to use the term mass until children are beyond the early years. In our everyday language we often refer to weight when we should be using the term mass. Adults need to deploy their vocabulary accurately using comparative language such as, 'The bucket of sand weighs *the same as* half a kilogramme.'

In the UK, imperial measurements are also used and can be seen on many food labels. 1 kg = 2.2 lb. British people usually weigh themselves on imperial scales and talk about stones and pounds. 1 st = 14 lb.

The concepts of weight and mass are inextricably linked to children's physical development. Children need to lift and move objects which feel heavy. They also need to develop a sense of balance, an awareness that one thing may feel heavier than another and also knowledge of their own physical strength. This goes hand in hand with a greater sense of proprioceptive and vestibular awareness.

The idea of weight and mass being different don't enter into most children's experiences. However, you can consider the idea of going up and down in a (fast) lift or riding on a roller coaster. When a lift goes down people feel lighter, but their mass doesn't change. Similarly, there is a perception of weightlessness at different times in a roller-coaster ride even though a person's mass hasn't changed.

These things might need to be explained if they are outside of children's day-to-day experiences. Playground equipment such as a swing, spinning wheel or seesaw will also exhibit forces that change the child's perception of weight (even though it doesn't actually change) without changing their mass. Understanding this is a challenge for many people, not just children.

Children need lots of play experiences around exploring mass and balancing objects of equivalent mass. Ensure that your outdoor provision has lots of opportunities for the children to lift, move and use objects of different mass that facilitate discussions about the concepts of heavy and light. Ensure standard measuring devices – such as standard weights and simple balance bucket weighing scales – are available outside.

Vocabulary

Balance, different, drop, equal, float, heavier, heaviest, heavy, kilo, kilogramme, light, lighter, lightest, load, loaded, mass, move, pounds, same, scales, sink, weight

Expressions

To weigh something up

To have something weighing on one's mind

As light as a feather

To have the weight of the world on your shoulders

To be worth your weight in gold

Idea 6.14 Non-standard objects that have different mass

Consider your range of loose parts in terms of the variety of sizes and how heavy and light objects feel when being lifted and moved. Some interesting approaches may include:

- Building up a collection of balls of different weights and sizes. Include ones that are big and light as well as some which are small and heavy.

- Acquiring tree stumps, logs and planks of wood which can be moved about. Every species of tree has unique properties, including the density of the wood which affects its mass and how heavy or light the wood feels. For this reason it is worthwhile sourcing big moveable wooden items from different species. Big hardwoods such as English oak (*Quercus robur*) and beech (*Fagus sylvatica*) feel comparatively heavier than similar sized pieces of softwood such as larch (*Larix decidua*) or Scots pine (*Pinus sylvestris*). Ask a tree surgeon, landscape gardener or forester about possible free sources of such wood. Sticks, cones and stones are also useful as they come in various different weights and sizes.

- Using PE equipment – balance boards, Saturn skippers, pogo sticks and giant tops all involve children using their body mass and comparative balance to work the equipment.

- Assembling different sizes of flowerpots for using as drums. Do the bigger, heavier containers produce deeper sounds?

- Putting pots and pans of different sizes and weights into an outdoor kitchen or music area. Explore the pitch of the sound in relation to how heavy a pan feels.

- Finding out if your trikes and bikes have significantly different weights. Some days just get the heavy bikes out, other days the light ones. Another day, go for a mix of heavy and light wheeled toys. Ask the children to find out more about heavy goods vehicles.

- Collecting a range of containers that help the children to establish which object feels the heaviest and lightest. It is tricky to compare the mass of two objects by holding them. Instead, encourage the children to pop objects into two similar bags or baskets and hold these. It makes the task slightly easier.

Idea 6.15 Twig mobiles

Create simple mobiles using twigs and Loom bands, elastic bands or hair ties. It involves quite a bit of manual dexterity. By using elastic attachments, the children can move the twigs into different places until they are balanced. It works best if the mobiles are begun as hanging structures and the children add to them gradually over time.

Idea 6.16 Hanging balancing pipe sculptures

It is possible to create a downward balancing structure using PVC piping and connectors. If a pipe is hung up at child height, the challenge is for them to attach more piping using the connectors to hold them in place. As the children build, they may see the need to keep each side balanced with regard to the mass of the pipes.

Idea 6.17 | Pulley systems

Pulleys are useful for exploring mass and weight as they involve lifting and moving items. The purpose of a pulley is to make this work easier. Children enjoy the pulling sensation when moving items: it is a novel way of investigating and learning about the comparative mass of different loads.

Try setting up a vertical pulley at a height which enables the children to pull a load up and down. Put up a rope line and attach a pulley or, alternatively, use a strong branch of a tree or a beam in a structure. Always double check that whatever the pulley is attached to will be strong enough to support the loads being lifted.

There are lots of investigations which can happen. For example:

- Use the pulley to lift different loads and compare ease of movement.

- Set up two pulleys beside each other so the children can directly compare the lifting of one object with another.

- Set up a double pulley, using two wheels to help lift a load. How does it feel lifting the same mass using a double pulley compared with a single one? Ask the children to count and compare the number of pulls taken to lift the load up into the air.

You can also try setting up pulleys between two different posts or branches to create a system for transporting loads horizontally across a space.

Be aware that pulleys are great for exploring changing forces but they don't change the mass. What changes is our perception of how heavy or light an object feels as pulleys change the force required to move it.

Idea 6.18 Bottle babies

I first heard about bottle babies via the Learning for Life blog.[1] The concept is believed to have been developed to help children with their communication skills. Bottle babies are two litre bottles which have been filled with objects of a child's choosing, topped up with coloured water and sealed. They are continuously available for the children to play with as they wish outside. They are useful as a non-standard unit of mass as lots of them are available and they can be used comparatively to weigh heavy items. For example, a log stump may feel the same weight as three bottle babies and a plank of wood may weigh less than three bottle babies – that is, lighter than the stump.

Idea 6.19 Stick swings

Set up a simple rope swing where a child has to sit on a stick with a rope secured through the middle. The children have to learn how to shift their mass to remain balanced on the swing. It is best to use a short fat stick that has been cut from a living tree so it won't break whilst in use.

Idea 6.20 Ordering stones and thinking about mass compared with size

Many children enjoy collecting rocks when out and about. Have fun talking about which one feels the heaviest and putting them in order. If tiny objects are found, discuss how the mass of little objects can be compared. Is size a reliable guide to how heavy something feels?

For children who are interested, challenge them to order their rocks in terms of mass. Get the children to compare the stones by holding them in a bag and estimating their mass. Next, encourage the children to consider how bucket or balance scales could help with this challenge. Be aware this is a complex problem so begin by comparing just two or three rocks.

Discuss which is the heaviest and which is the lightest. Is it true that the biggest stone is also the heaviest? Only put the rest in order if there is a desire to do so. If not, instead, challenge the children to find a rock which feels heavier than the heaviest rock or a stone that feels lighter than the lightest rock.

---

1 K. Corr, Outdoor play party – bottle babies, *Learning for Life* (31 January 2014). Available at: http://nosuchthingasbadweather.blogspot.co.uk/2014/01/outdoor-play-party-bottle-babies.html.

Learning to recognise and use a variety of scales

Idea 6.21 Different types of balance scales

Young children may be able to read a scale but conceptually they will find it challenging to understand the connection to weight and mass. Balance scales, sometimes called bucket scales, are more appropriate for young children. They enable comparative measures of weight to be undertaken using either standard or non-standard units of weight. There are many versions available so make sure you have ones which can cope with being used outside in all weathers.

Regardless of the type of scales you have, ensure you discuss with the children how they work and encourage them to experiment and explore at their own pace. Be prepared to model their use. Make sure that scales are always available for the children to use outside which can be moved to different places as they see fit to best meet their needs and interests. Have plenty of cones, stones, shells and other loose materials for the children to use as non-standard units of measure.

Idea 6.22 DIY balance scales

Simple balance scales can be made easily. Cut a straight stick from a living tree – the thicker the stick, the stronger it is likely to be. Cut a notch at either end. Hang the stick from a strong branch on a tree so that it is balanced. Use two bags or buckets of the same size as containers. The children can investigate what length of stick works best for comparing the mass of different objects.

An even simpler balance scale can be made from a coat hanger that has notches on either side. Or challenge the children to create a tiny balance scale for comparing the mass of very light objects.

It is worthwhile visiting play parks in your local area and finding out which ones have seesaws. These are essentially giant balance scales. The children can have fun discovering how many children it takes to lift a teacher into the air!

Idea 6.23 A mass-ive treasure hunt

Gold and other treasures are often weighed. This is one aspect of how their value is calculated. If there is a group of children interested in treasure or digging, then consider the following developments.

- Children enjoy wrapping rocks, stones and other objects in foil. They like to hide the 'treasure' around the outdoor space. Where could treasure be hidden, and why? Remind them that other children may want to find their hidden treasure.

- A dry stream or gravel pit can be turned into a gold panning area with the addition of sieves and fool's gold (iron pyrite).

- Set up a weighing centre where the children bring their finds, weigh them and have the weights noted. Adult assistance may be needed here. You could even offer money in relation to the weight of treasure found, like gold diggers in bygone days!

Idea 6.24 The larger the snowball, the more it weighs

Is this statement true? What do the children think? How can they work it out? What happens if holes are poked into the snowball?

Idea 6.25 A 'believe it or not' collection

Develop a collection of items that defy logic in terms of mass and size. These can be used to create a display. Ask the children, their parents/carers and others to contribute ideas and items. Here are some from my hoard:

- Pieces of material which are the same size but have a different mass. Lycra is surprisingly heavy compared to organza or silk.

- Balloons – a balloon that is blown up has the same mass as one which is not blown up.

- Large flight feathers from a gull, gathered from playing fields in late summer.

- A stone pine cone (*Pinus pinea*) and a sugar pine cone (*Pinus lambertiana*). The sugar pine cone is larger but feels lighter than the stone pine cone. But this may change if the cones are left to soak in water.

- A rock collection which includes a large piece of pumice rock. It feels so light!

- A large sponge – compare its mass when it is full of water to when it is wrung out.

Idea 6.26 Weighing stones

How many stones make one kilogramme? Create collections so everyone can compare the similarities and differences. Is it possible to find one stone which weighs a specific standard unit, such as one kilogramme? If so, keep hold of it as it is a special weighing stone. It can be marked and used with balance scales to measure the weight of other objects. This challenge works well on a stony beach, so take a set of balance scales for this purpose the next time you go.

Idea 6.27 A kilogramme of your favourite thing

What things do children like to collect? Encourage them to create collections of their favourite thing to make one kilogramme or half a kilogramme.

Hold a special kilogramme event where everyone's contribution can be put on display for others to see. This can be a good opportunity to involve families in bringing items from home.

Exploring length, distance, height, width and depth

Length, height, depth and width are all forms of distance or size: how far, long, near, short, wide, deep, narrow and so on. This aspect of measurement is closely linked to our bodies. The imperial measurement system uses feet and we still measure the height of a horse in hands. We can take steps or strides to measure distances covered. Children enjoy stories which cover aspects of size, such as 'Goldilocks and the Three Bears', 'Jack and the Beanstalk' and 'The Enormous Turnip', and these can be linked easily to outdoor play.

Conceptually, children have to learn about:

■ Accurate comparing of objects. It is easier to begin by comparing heights, such as two children, rather than horizontal lengths, such as two scarves laid on the ground beside each other.

■ Accurate measuring of items using non-standard units. Once a child can do this, standardised items can be introduced for measuring purposes.

■ Expressing length in pictorial form. This does not mean, at this stage, the accurate use of a ruler but more a chance to show a walking journey or to draw people of different heights and sizes. Experiences of scale are linked to this understanding and are discussed in Chapter 9.

- Conservation of length. A coiled rope appears shorter than the same length straightened out. Opportunities to manipulate rope and other flexible materials can help with understanding, especially if put in the context of a story or character, by using a puppet.

Children need play experiences to explore length and compare objects of different and equivalent lengths or sizes.[2] Trail making is a popular activity. Also, to begin to understand distance and moving from one place to another, the children need opportunities to move in different ways and to walk, cycle and use different forms of transport. Big distances are hard for children to understand and often they relate to them through the amount of time they feel it has taken to travel them. This can be subjective as an unfamiliar journey often feels longer than a known one. Thus, there are strong links with time and position, direction and movement, discussed in Chapters 7 and 10.

---

2 Do remember to supervise children when they are playing with rope and other long items to ensure they have been familiarised with all the resources and know the expectations around their use.

Distance is measured in metric units:

10 millimetres (mm) = 1 centimetre (cm)

100 cm = 1 metre (m)

1,000 m = 1 kilometre (km)

In the UK we still commonly use imperial measurements, which include:

12 inches = 1 foot

3 feet = 1 yard

1 furlong = one-eighth of a mile (220 yards)

8 furlongs = 1 mile (1,760 yards)

1 hand = 4 inches (for measuring the height of horses and ponies)

Vocabulary

Big, bigger than, centimetre, different, greater than, hand, height, inch, kilometre, large, length, less, little, long, longer, longest, macro, metre, micro, mile, more, same, short, shorter, shortest, small, smaller than, tiny, titchy, wide, wider, widest, width, yard

Expressions

Give him an inch and he will take a mile

As straight as the crow flies

Idea 6.28 Big and little

Very young children need opportunities to compare the sizes of different objects. For example:

- Finding the biggest and smallest tyres outside and putting them beside each other.

- Going on a hunt for a big stick and a small stick.

- Looking for the biggest and smallest vegetable that has been harvested.

- Playing matching games where big objects are paired with little ones. Use shells, stones, leaves and other natural materials available locally. Hide them in separate cotton bags for the children to guess which object is which.

Introduce comparative sizes of objects and the associated language. Use a variety of measuring vocabulary.

Idea 6.29 Big and little stick pictures

This activity reinforces the concept of comparative size. To begin with, let the children have lots of free-play experiences with sticks which have been cut to two lengths, with one exactly twice the length of the other (e.g. 30 cm and 60 cm).

Next, challenge the children to work in pairs to create one small and one large picture or shape that are exactly the same. For example, if one child makes a house with small sticks, their partner needs to make the same house but with large sticks. Take photos to record the results. This is a good self-directed activity for older children.

This activity can be extended using non-standard lengths of sticks so the children have to grade the materials according to their own judgement.

Idea 6.30 A hand-sized scavenger hunt

Set up a scavenger hunt where the children have to find objects of certain sizes. For example:

- A stick smaller than my hand.
- A blade of grass longer than my little finger.
- A leaf as wide as my hand span.
- A nut the size of my thumbnail.
- A stone which fits inside my hand.

The children can draw around their hands on a piece of card (e.g. the back of a cereal packet). The objects can be glued or taped onto their own cardboard hands to display their findings.

When organising a scavenger hunt with young children, there are alternatives to a written list, including:

- Adults can tell each child or group what to collect. Once a child has brought the object back to show the adult, the next clue is read out.
- Stick examples on a portable whiteboard or blackboard that is displayed outside.
- Prepare laminated photographs of objects which can be used for various activities.

Idea 6.31 A comparative competition

This challenge reinforces concepts of size such as bigger than, smaller than, longer than and so on. The aim is for the children to invent their own competition and come up with comparative measurements to explore. For example:

- Which is the biggest and smallest door in the school?

- Which is the widest and narrowest window?

- Which is the tallest and smallest plant they can find?

- Which is the longest and shortest way to the play park when following the paths?

The aim is to see how many questions can be created that are possible to investigate. The children can then have fun exploring their own suggestions and sharing the results. It is also an opportunity to involve parents and visitors to your setting – they can be encouraged to think about comparative challenges too. The questions and results can all be recorded so the children can see what everyone has learnt.

Idea 6.32 Stick line-up

This game helps the children to understand a variety of measurement concepts: big and small, wide and narrow, straight and bent, and ordering according to size.

Each child has to find a stick or twig. Each child in turn lays their stick on a light coloured cloth or sheet. The challenge is to put their stick in the correct place so the sticks are arranged in order from smallest to largest.

This is a good opportunity to introduce comparative language. The non-uniformity of the sticks helps to facilitate mathematical discussions around whether a stick with a bend in it is longer than one which is straight. A piece of string can be useful to help the children make these measurements. Also, some children may feel that size could be about width rather than length.

Idea 6.33 | The natural comparison challenge

This activity is a useful way of introducing or reinforcing vocabulary related to size and measurement. You need to have a selection of word cards prepared which are related to length: shorter, longer, bigger, smaller, wider, narrower, taller.

If a child finds something of interest outside such as a stone, twig or leaf, then they may wish to put it on a white interest sheet (see Idea 11.10) for further discussions or games. There is a challenge that can be introduced at this point. Any child who wishes to be involved picks a word card (e.g. 'smaller'). They now look at the objects on the sheet and have to find a smaller example of one of the objects. Once this is found, it can be placed beside their original object.

After a while, re-gather the children together and have a look at the discoveries. Encourage them to use the comparison words from the cards as they talk about their found 'treasures'. This further reinforces the comparative words. Were any cards not used? Is it possible to find examples for the unused words?

Idea 6.34 | Investigating lines, patterns and quantities

Investigate the number of bricks or other objects needed to make a line from one place to another. What other objects can be lined up, counted and used for non-standard measuring?

Have fun estimating quantities of natural objects in relation to length. For example:

- The length of a person lying on the ground as measured with pine cones. How many cones will be needed to create an outline of a child's body? If children can't lie still for long enough, then chalk around them first and add the objects afterwards.

- How many shells will fit on a squiggle drawn in the sand on a beach?

- Which feather is the same size as my hand (and is this the length or width of my hand)? This is great to do on playing fields and parks in late summer when the gulls have moulted.

Idea 6.35 How big is a hug?

- Link hands and find out how many children are needed to make a line across the outdoor area. How many children would it take to hug your school building?

- Use a measuring tape to measure the girth of trees and other objects outside. How many children are needed to hug the biggest tree? Do big trees need a bigger hug than smaller trees? Is it possible to find a tree with a girth that is the same size as a hug from one child?

- What other features can be measured with a hug?

Measuring when out and about

We are always trying to put maths in to our little trips to the woods. We love to find things to measure and then find out its length in children. The fun bit is when we can only use half a child.

I always have a tape measure in my bag. We have quite a bit of snow here in the winter. We were walking in the lava fields where there are a quite a few crevasses. Some of them were filled with snow but had little holes. We couldn't feel how deep they were so we managed to slide the tape measure down and measure how deep it was. As numbers don't always make sense to all the children, we changed the numbers into the names of children. So two-and-a-half children was the depth of the crevasse. That they understood and thought was funny.

Unnur Henrys, pre-school teacher, Iceland

Idea 6.36 Skip, wrap and roll

When children play with skipping ropes they learn that whether they jump over it, wrap it up or move and shake it like a snake on the ground, it still stays the same length. Using the fixed sizes of bandages and ribbons can also help to reinforce conservation of length. Let the children roll them up, roll them out, weave them together, compare lengths and so on.

Idea 6.37 Throwing things

Throw objects and measure how far away they land from where you threw them. Have a range of measuring tools on offer and let the children decide which is the best tool to use for the job. How far can they throw:

- A welly boot.
- A flying disc.
- A paper aeroplane.
- Any other suggestions made by the children.

Discuss beforehand whether there is anything which should not be thrown, even it may be very interesting to do so.

Consider how an object is thrown – for example, is it easier to throw a spinning object like a flying disc overarm, underarm or with a flick?

For more accuracy, with some objects you may want to:

- Throw them to a friend (e.g. a flying disc).
- Get them to land in a bucket placed on the ground.
- Throw them through something, such as a hoop that has been hung up.
- Aim at a target, such as concentric circles or a series of lines chalked on the ground.

Idea 6.38 Kicking

Kicking is an activity that can be used for comparing distances. It could include:

■ Kicking a football. What is the furthest distance from the net from which a child can score a goal?

■ Drop-kicking balls high into the air. Is it possible to work out how high a ball has been kicked without it getting stuck somewhere?

Idea 6.39 Rolling challenges

Investigate how far two different cars, balls or other rolling objects will travel down a piece of guttering and onto the ground. Encourage the children to come up with their own methods of measuring the distance travelled. Does the mass of an object affect the distance it travels? Or is it all about the length or gradient of the slope?

Idea 6.40 Pine cone boules

Cones are very good for introducing children to the French game of boules. It is best played on a flat surface. Each child who wants to play needs to find two large cones – the bigger the better – and mark them in some way. You also need a tiny cone such as from a larch (*Larix decidua*). This one is thrown a short distance. The challenge is for each child to take turns to throw their pine cone as close as possible to the little cone. Use string to compare distances from the little cone to the children's cones.

Idea 6.41 Jumping distances

■ Decide how many paving slabs it is possible to jump over when walking along a pavement.

■ Compare the length of a jump starting from standing still with one where the children can take a run-up and then jump.

■ Draw a 'V' on the ground. The children start close to the point and take turns jumping over the V. As they take a go, they gradually move further along the V so they have to jump further to reach the other line.

Idea 6.42 | Developing the concept of one metre

Measuring sticks are ideal for children to use in their free play to help them develop their understanding of one metre. Having a stack of one metre sticks available allows for measuring longer distances and creating shapes and outlines, the perimeter of which can be calculated easily by counting the number of sticks laid down end to end.

The children can estimate how long one metre is by laying objects on the ground and then comparing their line with the cut stick. They usually need to be shown how to place objects so they touch each other. A good way to introduce this is through a simple game with a dice. The children take turns to roll the dice. They then have to lay the corresponding number of objects along the stick. The winner is the one who adds the final object to make one metre.

Another challenge is to ask pairs of children to make one metre using one type of natural material such as shells. Ask each pair to count the number of shells used. There will be a range of responses which can lead to some interesting discussions about why this is so. The next challenge is to see if each pair can create one metre using a specified number of shells (e.g. twenty shells).

CHAPTER 7

Time

Seasonal and daily variations in the natural world give a multisensory indication that changes are happening through time. Day and night bring a familiar rhythm that can provide consistency and security to children. Routines are also governed by time; these are discussed in Chapter 12. Yet developing a sense of time can be a challenge. It is an abstract concept that takes a lot of practice to master, and the desire to acquire the skill and understanding. Furthermore, children's developmental concept of longer time intervals, such as seasons, is limited by their time on the planet. Thus, children need lots of experiences to develop a sense of what time encompasses, including opportunities to:

■ Sequence events in their lives such as daily routines and longer time periods which include what happened yesterday and what will happen tomorrow.

■ Record and talk about events over longer time frames: weeks, months and seasons.

■ Experience time through estimating and measuring specific intervals of time.

■ Engage in conversations about time and develop the extensive range of vocabulary and use of language associated with it.

There are a lot of skills involved in understanding time. It involves the children:

■ Knowing and being able to use the vocabulary associated with time.

■ Measuring time as it moves forwards or backwards (e.g. when a countdown happens).

■ Sequencing events in time and being aware of the order in which events happen.

■ Being able to log as well as measure time with a variety of different equipment.

■ Understanding duration – how long a minute or other time intervals are.

■ Being aware of seasonal changes taking place and longer measurements of time.

■ Recognising and reading digital and analogue time.

It is tempting to focus on children's ability to tell the time using digital and analogue clocks. However, this should not be confused with a child having a well-developed concept of time that comes from sequencing events, measuring time intervals and being involved in sustained shared conversations and thinking about time.

Vocabulary

After, afternoon, almost, analogue, anticlockwise, before, century, clock, clockwise, date, day, digital, evening, fast, forever, hour, how long, later, midday, midnight, minute, moment, month, morning, nearly, never, next, night, noon, now, pendulum, quickly, season, second, slow, soon, sunrise, sunset, then, week, year

Spring, summer, autumn, winter

Monday, Tuesday, Wednesday, Thursday, Friday, Saturday, Sunday

January, February, March, April, May, June, July, August, September, October, November, December

Expressions

A stitch in time saves nine

Hang on a minute

Wait a moment

Idea 7.1 Measuring time

Have a range of timers, stopwatches and clocks which can be used outside on a regular basis in all sorts of situations. Adults may need to model and show the children how to use the different timers for activities such as:

- Observing how long it takes for snow or ice to melt. How can the children devise a fair test?

- Monitoring the length of time it takes for a bucket of dry sand to pass through a sieve.

- Playing Poohsticks. Drop sticks into a river or stream on one side of a bridge and count how long each one takes before emerging on the other side of the bridge.

- Measuring how long it takes for a person to negotiate an obstacle course or run up a hill.

- Timing a dance routine or impromptu music rendition.

- Timing activities such as jumping and to encourage the development of pace.

- Timing and counting laps when racing on wheeled toys.

- Using sand-timers and rockers – these are often portable, robust and waterproof. They are useful for turn taking outside, and the children quickly learn to do this independently.

Ask parents and children to donate used parking tickets which have a time printed on them. These can be used with wheeled toys. Any bicycle left parked in the wrong place can be given a fine or clamped and taken to the 'bike pound'. Children may have to pay money for the toy to be reclaimed.

Idea 7.2 Pendulums

Pendulums can be used to measure time – many traditional clocks rely on pendulums to keep accurate time. A pendulum is a rod with a weight at the end. The length of the rod affects the speed at which the pendulum oscillates. Pendulums have practical uses outside. Adults can encourage the children to vary the length of their pendulum and to observe the consequence on the rate of oscillation.

Activities involving pendulums include:

- Painting or water play using a pendulum. This can be set up on a tripod or overhead line of rope over a sheet or asphalt – a surface on which the oscillating patterns can be observed. Put a small hole in a plastic milk bottle and hang it up on a piece of thin rope. In order for the children to adjust the length of the rope, it is easiest if it is set up on a swivel pulley system.

- Piñata. This traditional game, which is popular in Mexico, involves filling a pottery, papiermâché or cloth container with sweets or small objects and hanging it up on a string. People are blindfolded and have to try to hit the piñata to break it and release the contents. The concept can be adapted for children by having soft items hung up that they can hit and then watch as they swing.

- Rope swings. Children love to swing and in doing so they can directly experience a pendulum oscillating. By varying the length of the rope the oscillation can be long and slow or short and fast. When setting up a rope swing, ask for advice from the children about the length of the rope needed. If you have hammocks the length of the ropes attaching them to the trees can be adjusted.

Idea 7.3 Old and discarded clocks

Hoard unwanted watches and interesting old clocks, both digital and analogue, for the children to use in their free play. Save plastic watches from crackers and so on. Let the children take apart old clocks to see what is inside the casing and how they work. An adult may need to unscrew the fastenings a little to get the children started. Remember to remove batteries and cables from electric clocks.

Idea 7.4 Visiting places where time matters

A visit to a train or bus station, or even an airport, is fascinating. Encourage the children to listen to the information being relayed over the loudspeaker. It is even better if the children have to catch a bus or take a train somewhere.

Idea 7.5 Time lapse photos and videos

Many children do not notice or readily see the changes happening in nature. There are many examples of time lapse videos on YouTube, such as 'One Year in 40 Seconds',[1] which provide good illustrations of the changing seasons and natural events to help children see life cycles and slower changes taking place.

A time lapse activity can help the children to look and see. It involves taking photos of something within a set time period (e.g. once an hour or once a day). Good examples include:

- A dandelion changing into a dandelion clock.

- A fast-growing plant beginning to bloom.

- A snowball melting or a patch of grass growing.

- A spider spinning a web.

You can download time lapse apps for tablets which enable you to set up your device so photos are taken at timed intervals. There are also sports coaching apps which allow you to replay short videos in slow motion to evaluate techniques. Children enjoy seeing themselves move in slow motion.

Idea 7.6 Seasonal activities and food

Spend time outside throughout the year undertaking seasonal activities and celebrations. There are many books which give ideas for celebratory activities outdoors. For example:

- Plant seeds of local produce in spring to harvest in summer and autumn. Take photos and keep a diary of their growth from germination through to harvest.

- Hold a snow festival – have resources and ideas ready to grab and go when the snow arrives.

- Go for regular walks and look for signs of the different seasons.

- Learn to tell the time with a dandelion clock. Blow the seed heads off a dandelion, and each time you blow say, '1 o'clock', '2 o'clock' and so on. When no more seeds are left on the dandelion, you have reached the correct dandelion time!

---

1 See: https://www.youtube.com/watch?v=lmIFXIXQQ_E.

Idea 7.7 Rearing animals

Watching animals grow and change helps children to understand life cycles and develop another sense of what time means. Even if your nursery does not have hens, fertile chicken eggs can be bought and hatched. If possible, keep the chickens afterwards, but if not, check that they can be returned with the incubator to a reputable supplier. Frog-spawn is also exciting to keep. The Froglife website provides helpful advice about collecting and caring for spawn.[2]

Care of the animals is of paramount importance: routines to ensure their well-being, as well as that of the children in your care, matter. It is also important that such activities are highlighted and that the children know what is happening and why. It is a time-based celebration of life!

Idea 7.8 Learning about day and night

Children know about day and night but do not necessarily make the connection with time. It is worthwhile organising a couple of events at suitable times of the year and involving families in the activities.

- Hold a 'dawn break' party just before sunrise so the children can witness dawn breaking. Arrange an outdoor breakfast with hot drinks and pancakes or warm cereal, such as porridge.

- A 'sunset' party enables the children to witness the change from day to night as the sun sinks. Take photos and notice the changing light levels.

- Go for a walk in the daytime and repeat the same walk as part of a sunset party after dark, so the children can compare and contrast the experience.

2 See: http://www.froglife.org/info-advice/spawn-tadpoles-habitat/.

- Share some ideas for exploring the dark with parents so the children have opportunities to enjoy this time outside school too.[3]

- Talk about events which happen during the day and compare these to events which happen at night.

Telling the time

The activities below are aimed at children who are keen to learn to tell the time. Remember that all of the previous experiences and language development opportunities outlined earlier in this chapter are of paramount importance in developing children's concept of time. Without such formative experiences they will struggle when working through tasks associated with telling the time.

Idea 7.9 What time is it, Mr Wolf?

One child is the wolf who stands at the opposite end of the playground to the rest of the group. The group chants, 'What time is it, Mr Wolf?' The wolf turns around and says a time, such as '3 o'clock'. The group takes that number of steps towards the wolf. The chant is repeated and the wolf turns around and calls out another time. When someone gets close to the wolf, the wolf can shout 'Dinner time!' and chase the group back to the starting line. Then another child becomes the wolf and the game begins again.

Idea 7.10 Making an outdoor clock

Ask older children about how they could make a large clock outside that is big enough to use for a group game. What materials do they need, and how will they make it? Ask them to think about what makes their clock especially suitable for being outside. This activity is useful for assessing the children's understanding of what a clock is.

When the clock is made, play a few simple games and sing songs which involve the children moving the hands of the clock – for example, sing 'Hickory Dickory Dock' and act out the nursery rhyme around the clock.

Once the children are proficient at making a large group clock, they can be encouraged to make their own smaller versions.

---

3 This blog post features a selection of experiences to offer young children to help them enjoy and learn about the dark: J. Robertson, Play in the dark – 10 ideas, *Creative Star Learning* (3 November 2013). Available at: http://creativestarlearning.co.uk/early-years-outdoors/play-in-the-dark-10-ideas/.

Idea 7.11 Hoop clocks

For this activity, each child or pair needs a hoop, chalk, numbered stones, or similar, and two sticks (for the hour and minute hands). The hoop is placed on the ground and twelve numbered stones are placed around the hoop by the children. The adult can then ask the children to make different times, such as '1 o'clock', 'Three hours later' and so on. The children use the sticks to make the time. Make sure you have a clock face handy to show children the time and allow them to correct their mistakes.

Idea 7.12 Human clocks

Start by getting the children to rock from foot to foot whilst slowly chanting, 'Tick, tock, tick, tock. I'm a ticking human clock. What time is it?' The adult calls out a time, such as '5 o'clock'. The children make the time with their arms. (Remember it will look back to front if you are standing in front of the children.) Ensure you have a clock face on hand so the children can check and correct their answers. Repeat the chant before calling out each time. This also works as an activity undertaken in pairs with one child moving the arms of their partner to the correct position.

Idea 7.13 Time line-up

Stick images of clock faces and/or digital clocks showing different times onto laminated cards. Give one card to each child in the group and ask them to line up in order as you read aloud or make up a story which goes through a typical day. Begin with hours and move on to half past, quarter to, quarter past and so on as the children's understanding grows.

Idea 7.14 Clockwise and anticlockwise

Clockwise and anticlockwise are abstract concepts that need plenty of reinforcement in different situations to help the children understand them.

- Look for opportunities to mention the direction in which children are running or moving when playing – for example, 'I saw you spinning clockwise when on the grass.'

- When the children are moving objects, make comments such as, 'Try turning the milk crate anticlockwise to make it fit on top of the other one.'

- During circle games, refer to objects being passed clockwise or anticlockwise around the circle or reinforce the direction when turn taking.

Using time in a play-based context

Following a child's interest in horses, we had a horse jumping competition. We set up some jumps from crates and guttering. As the children were busy having a practice, I made up a simple scoreboard with each child's name.

We had a stopwatch for timing the race and an iPad for taking photos and filming. All of the children wanted to have a go, but first they had to find their name on the scoreboard. They listened to how to use the technology and then off they trotted.

On completion of the race, they had a look at their score and some children could identify the numerals. All but two children wanted to have a go at writing their score up on the scoreboard. Children took turns and cheered each other on. At the end we had a medal ceremony – I quickly attached a leaf to a piece of string.

After this activity, the children continued to use loose parts to make other races and obstacle courses. They asked for the iPad to time each other. This was completely initiated by them. The children used the vocabulary of time (seconds), even though they did not truly understand this concept yet.

Rachel Besford, nursery teacher, Little Explorers Outdoor Pre-School, Cornwall

CHAPTER 8

Pattern

Patterns are repeating sequences or arrangements of objects, numbers, actions and events that systematically follow a given rule. Maths is underpinned by patterns which can be seen all around us. Most children and adults are pattern-seekers because patterns help us to understand and make sense of the world, providing order and routine. When we discover a pattern we make a connection and recognise a structure or rule. We can represent patterns in different ways – through numbers or other symbols. Then we can make assumptions and predictions and have fun exploring what happens when we do this.

Patterns come in many guises:

- Number patterns. There is a logic to our number system and thus many patterns emerge purely from exploring number, such as the Fibonacci sequence. Encouraging children to develop an awareness of patterns in number relationships helps to develop their confidence in manipulating numbers. The visual and spatial appeal of patterns facilitates our ability to understand number.

- Logic patterns. These use different attributes including shape, colour, size and line. Symmetry and tessellation are forms of patterns.

- Word patterns. All languages have patterns within them based upon their lettering or symbols. Rhymes are examples of word patterns.

- There are intrinsic links between mark making and pattern work, particularly in relation to line patterns.

- Patterns which are heard or felt such as music, dance and sound.

- Patterns in nature. These include fractals (like snowflakes), the arrangement of petals and leaves on plants, the markings on animals and the textural patterns in rocks, spiders' webs and honeycomb. It also includes patterns of time, such as the seasons and the sequencing of events.

- Pattern is a visual element of art and design. Formal or random patterns are found in all cultures. Patterns decorate and embellish bodies in the form of tattoos. Repeated patterns can be found in fabric design and knitwear.

- Pattern in the built environment. Buildings and other man-made structures have patterns inherent in their design detail.

For children to understand pattern, there are a number of important developmental steps. Firstly, there is the awareness of what a pattern actually is. This goes beyond recognition of simple relational terms such as big and small to an identifiable repeating sequence, thus at least three sequential items are required.

Secondly, an understanding of attributes is needed. These are the characteristics that are used to identify an object and which can be used for comparative purposes. These may include number, shape, colour, size, texture, position and quantity. Patterns can alternate between two attributes or two objects (e.g. big, small, big, small; leaf, stone, leaf, stone). Children will naturally recognise and explore such a pattern. It can be harder for them to arrange three or more distinctly different items which are then repeated (e.g. leaf, stone, stick, leaf, stone, stick) and this is where saying the pattern out loud as you look across and 'read' it is helpful.

Thirdly, in order to recognise patterns in their different guises – and to move on to copying, adding to and creating their own sequences – children need experience of, and to explore and repeatedly create, a wide range of patterns. Their purpose, complexities, similarities and differences are subjects for endless discussion. In due course their pattern work will become more complex.

Adults need to understand the different elements of pattern making so they can extend children's knowledge and understanding of patterns in all their forms. This includes opportunities to:

- Explore patterns in nature and the local environment.
- Order objects.
- Recognise, copy and create repeating sequences, expanding patterns and symmetry.
- Experience first-hand cyclical patterns, such as rotational symmetry, and sequences which form a closed repeating pattern as opposed to a linear or block pattern.
- Play strategy games where recognising and using patterns is a problem-solving strategy.
- Develop the language of description, position and movement which pattern work involves.

It is also important to integrate number into pattern work. For example:

- Ensure the children have lots of opportunities to organise sets of objects into different numbers. Organising groups of objects – such as splitting twelve objects into two groups of six, or into four groups of three – helps children learn a range of numeracy skills, such as conservation of number and aspects of division and fractions.
- Identify odd and even numbers.
- Count in twos, fives and tens when appropriate to do so.
- Look for and use arrays of different sorts – that is, organise objects into patterns which aid basic concepts such as addition, subtraction, multiplication and division.
- Play games and provide materials which help the children to develop their knowledge and understanding of the tens' complement (i.e. pairs of numbers which add up to ten).
- Introduce doubles and use the concept to make addition and subtraction easier. Doubles have a pattern that I have found children tend to pick up more easily than other number bonds, especially when they can see a concrete or pictorial representation, such as the dot pattern on a pair of dice.
- Use known patterns, such as the dots on dominoes and dice, Numicon colours and layouts, to help the children recognise quantities.

Vocabulary

After, again, balance, before, curved, decrease, different, finish, in and out, in-between, increase, lines, match, middle, next to, pattern, puzzle, repeat, round, same, sequences, smooth, spiral, spots, start, strategy, stripes, under and over, up and down, wavy, zigzag

When the children are sufficiently interested in patterns, introduce them to the following extension possibilities.

Idea 8.1 Making a single line pattern more complex

- A child may have laid a trail on the ground with sticks arranged end to end. You could ask if a stone could be placed in-between each stick to see if this changes the trail in any way.

- If a child has put out number pebbles in order, then a soft toy or puppet could have a look and request that they turn over every other number, so that only odd numbers are showing.

- With patterns which have some items that are the same (e.g. stick, stick, stick, stone, stick, stick, stick, stone), encourage the children to look for the smaller repeated chunk.

Idea 8.2 Extend a single line pattern

Patterns do not have to be developed and extended in a horizontal line. When playing a game of dominoes, part of the fun is that the dominoes can be placed in ways which mean the pattern develops to the left or right of the first piece, then up or down. Simple extensions include:

- Creating block patterns. If a child has laid out a cone, stone, cone, stone pattern, this line can be used to create a block. Ask the children if they can continue the block pattern.

- Making a rule when playing a stick game that every time a stick is placed on the ground, it must create a corner with the stick it touches. This can be developed even further by using rainbow maths sticks (see Idea 8.28).[1]

- Challenging the children to present quantities that represent numbers in different ways. This is where arrays come into their own in terms of creating patterns. Using a tens frame may result in many different layouts to represent a given number.

1 See also: J. Robertson, Rainbow maths sticks, *Creative Star Learning* (8 April 2014). Available at: http://creativestarlearning.co.uk/maths-outdoors/rainbow-maths-sticks/.

Explore patterns in nature and the environment

Rather than simply asking the children to look for patterns outside, it can be more interesting for them to consider the meaning and purpose of patterns and find out their preferences. Collections can be created from objects, photos, rubbings and drawings made by the children. They can also make patterns using different materials.

Idea 8.3 Sandpit patterns

- ■ Have dry sand available for pouring through sieves and funnels onto wet sand. Enjoy watching the patterns form and have fun mixing the sands together.

- ■ Use a pendulum on a tripod for a bigger pattern. Attach a little bag of sand to some rope. Make a little hole in the bottom of the bag. Swing it back and forth to make patterns on a tarp or cloth. Investigate what happens to the patterns created when the length of the rope is shortened or made longer.

- ■ Go miniature. Ensure there are little objects available for miniature pattern making on a sandy surface.

Idea 8.4 Footprints in the sand

Make footprints in the sand at the beach. Children notice this spontaneously and enjoy creating trails. Experiment with patterns based on different ways of moving on sand (e.g. skipping, jumping, walking backwards or like a duck or hopping).

- ■ Can the children retrace their steps and put their feet carefully back into their prints? Is it possible to count the number of footprints you make by walking in them again?

- ■ What do the children notice when they try to put their feet in someone else's prints?

- ■ Where is the best place on the beach to make footprints and why?

- ■ Use language such as bigger, smaller, curved sides, symmetrical, longer, shorter, wider, narrower.

The focus on footprint patterns can be further extended:

■ Draw around feet and compare this to the pattern of the footprints in the sand.

■ Get the children to cut out their footprint and use it as a counting viewer.[2]

■ The children may notice and wish to explore patterns made by animals in the sand. Can they find dog paw prints or bird tracks?

■ What other objects can be pressed into sand to make a print? Make up a guessing game based around the prints.

Idea 8.5 Drippy castles

Make mud into a gloopy texture and encourage the children to squeeze this through their hands to create drippy spirals and mounds. What is the best consistency for making spiralling mounds? What other patterns can be made with drippy mud? Does it matter what surface the mud falls onto?

Idea 8.6 Water and snow patterns

■ Have sticks and stirrers in the water tray for stirring water and making patterns.

■ Make a small hole in the bottom of a bucket. Fill it with water and let the children take turns to carry it to make water trails.

■ Use hoses, squirty bottles, syringes and watering cans to make water patterns on asphalt.

■ Experiment with different sizes of brush for mark making using water on the ground and walls outside – from brooms to small paintbrushes.

■ Dip different types of tyre into water and roll them on concrete. Can the children work out which tread pattern belongs to which tyre?

■ Use syringes and coloured water to make detailed line patterns. Create pattern trails for each other to follow.

---

2 For more on this technique see J. Robertson, Daisy footprints – maths outdoors, *Creative Star Learning* (10 July 2013). Available at: http://creativestarlearning.co.uk/early-years-outdoors/daisy-footprints/.

Idea 8.7 — Fence weaving

Weave ribbons and strips of natural or man-made materials into fences. Use just two colours and watch the patterns develop. Have some patterns ready-made for the children to continue and also encourage them to leave space for others to continue their ideas. Provide provocations – for example, if the children are only weaving horizontally, show them how to weave vertically. Then bring in diagonals. What about a symmetrical pattern? Can the children create a ribbon spiral?

Idea 8.8 — Musical patterns outside

If I hear a child tapping the ground or a fence with a stick, I echo the rhythm with a stick, or by clapping my hands or stamping my feet. This often leads to a lot of counting, beating and tapping. If other children want to join in, bear in mind the following:

- Consider which objects make good sounds or noises. Sticks are generally good and loud. Stones are quieter. With a friend or adult, the children can copy or echo simple sound patterns or simply tap together in time.

- The children can jump or move in time to a stick being tapped. Marching activities work well – left, right, left, right, etc. These help to develop a sense of beat.

- Tap out rhythms with sticks and other found objects. Remember to include contrasts such as high and low pitches, fast and slow, loud and quiet.

- There are lots of rhythm games and activities which can be undertaken outside with natural materials. Look in music books and adapt the activities.

- Encourage the children to represent their musical patterns by mark making and developing visual representations of the sounds.

- Have a look at the stick counting activities in Idea 3.19.

Idea 8.9 Using the environment to develop dance patterns

Dances are repeated physical patterns and sequences. It is possible to use the environment to link symbols for objects to moves in dance. The children can have fun being creative here.

- When passing a lamp post, lift your hands up high and straight.
- When under a tree, wave your hands high in the air.
- Make an 'H' sign with your hands at every fire hydrant.

When staying within one space, patterns can be created using symbols. For example, on a beach you and the children can draw symbols in the sand to represent certain movements. For example:

- Do a star jump when a cross is drawn.
- Turn around when a spiral is drawn.
- Walk in a wavy way when a squiggle is drawn.

Idea 8.10 Group patterns

Let the children make group patterns (e.g. a large square, a small circle) by holding hands or by standing, sitting in a circle, stepping in and out, and so on. Encourage the children to come up with their own ideas for group patterns (e.g. lift hands up, lift hands down). Introduce a puppet who can give instructions – such as, 'Red Fox says lift your hands up' or 'Red Fox says put your hands down and step back out.'

Games such as 'duck, duck, goose' have a distinct pattern. Encourage the children to change the rules and see how this affects the way the game is played.

Idea 8.11 Ball bouncing patterns

If you are throwing, rolling or catching a ball with a child or group of children, then verbalise the patterns or actions – such as, 'roll, bounce, pass'. Build this up into pattern work by encouraging the children to copy each other (e.g. 'bounce, pass; bounce, pass').

Challenge the children to invent simple bouncing patterns – this can either be done alone or in pairs. How can this be extended to include throwing, rolling or other ways of moving the ball between two or more people? Very often children who enjoy football or rugby will see the value of passing patterns, especially if they lead to scoring a goal or a try.

Idea 8.12 | Rub those patterns

Take rubbings of different objects in the local area as well as in the designated outdoor area. Paper often gets wet outside so try using the following materials:

- Calico cotton, available from most haberdashery shops and departments. Experiment with berries, leaves from plants, mud and so on to see what works well for rubbing. This can be particularly effective if the children have added lines of masking tape to the cotton beforehand, which can be removed afterwards to reveal line patterns (see Idea 8.22).

- Aluminium foil. Press this down onto different surfaces and gently rub to get the impression. This is ideal for rainy days or to create textured patterns for space themed constructions.

- Clay. This can be pressed onto different objects or features and carefully removed to reveal the imprint.

Can your children work out which rubbed pattern comes from which object? This can be surprisingly tricky to ascertain!

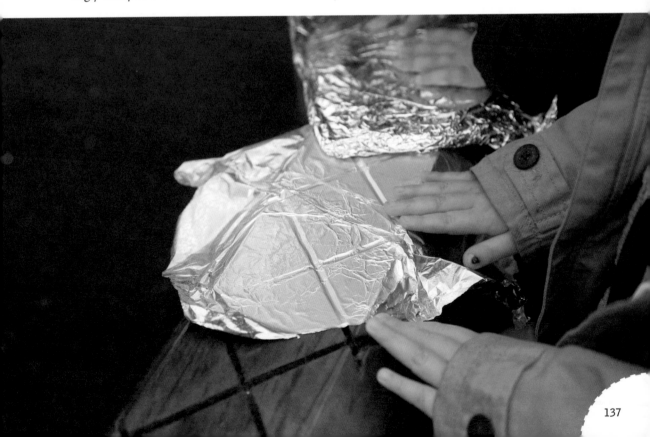

Idea 8.13 | Paving slab patterns

Some children love to move along a pavement in different ways. Draw attention to the pattern they are making. A common one is hopscotch: two feet, one foot, two feet, one foot. Paving slab patterns are ideal for inventing or extending games.

■ Is it possible to only step on the slabs whilst walking from one lamp post to another? What happens if you step on a crack or line?

■ Is it possible to jump on alternate slabs? Do you think you will take more or fewer steps than if you walked normally?

■ Can you hopscotch from one lamp post to another? (See Idea 3.20 for more hopscotch suggestions.)

■ Use chalk to extend the patterns seen in paving slabs and for the children to create their own.

A teacher of a class of five-year-olds had placed chalk on the ground outside her class. One child decided to use the chalk to colour in the tiles on the ground. The pattern was not explicit but clearly the child had chosen her colours carefully and had spent considerable time on this activity.

To build upon this work, the teacher suggested that the wooden building blocks from the classroom had a similar shape. She wondered whether the child would be able to use the blocks to copy the tiling pattern she had made on the ground in chalk. From here the child experimented with other tiling layouts that were possible with the same shapes.

Idea 8.14 Nature kebabs

When on a walk or in a natural space, the children can collect finds and thread them onto a thin, straight stick. Often the children will choose to collect what interests them. You can model patterns to give them some inspiration, such as alternating leaf colour, species or size.

Idea 8.15 Leaf bunting

Collected leaves can be pegged up on a piece of twine or string. Deciding the order or sequence is an important part of pattern making and the children will have plenty of ideas. It can be helpful to have spare string available so that plenty of children can be involved should they so wish. It makes a lovely, temporary visual display. To make it more permanent, the children can press their leaves first so they are dry and flat. Lines of leaves can also be hung vertically too.

Idea 8.16 | What patterns exist in nature?

Look out for patterns within the natural world such as on pine cones, swirling patterns in water, birds migrating and so on.

- Have magnifiers, handheld microscopes and mirrors to aid investigations and observations of minute patterns and details.

- What is the smallest natural pattern that can be found?

- What are the biggest or most frequent patterns observed in nature? Develop a bank of possible ideas and consider the function of patterns.

- Encourage the children to take photos and create galleries or albums based upon their ideas for how to sort the patterns.

Idea 8.17 | Spirals

If a child has a particular interest in a pattern, then use this as a focus for learning about the wider purpose and application of pattern. For example, a spiral has many practical functions:

- It enables an animal or plant (or part of either) to fit neatly into a small space. To illustrate, if you have a length of rope the children can compare the space it takes up when rolled up in a spiral to when it is uncoiled.

- Spirals offer protection: hedgehogs roll into a ball and millipedes coil up. The exterior protects what is inside.

- It is a strong shape – think of the strength of a spider's web. Look at the power of waves as they curl and crash upon the beach. Watch a tornado spin through the air.

- It is a good defence. Horns, such as ram's horns, grow in a spiral – these are used when fighting or to protect the animal if threatened.

- Lots of animals curl up to keep warm: mice, foxes – even pet cats and dogs.

- Spirals in nature can represent a form of growth. Spirals often grow as a living creature does – think of snails' shells and seahorses' tails. Even the universe is an expanding spiral.

- Spirals are useful for gripping or holding on to something. Octopuses use their spiral shaped legs to feel their way and hold on to aquatic plants and other objects. Monkeys use their tails to curl around branches. An elephant can pick up logs by curling its trunk around them.

- Spirals are beautiful and can be seen in the growth patterns of cones and flowers such as roses, daises and sunflowers.

- Make spirals by moving a stick round and round in a puddle or by letting water flow down a sink when the plug is removed. Throw seeds such as sycamore wings into the air and watch them spiral back down. What other spirals can the children create?

Idea 8.18 Exploring pattern through environmental art

The seven visual elements of art have strong links with maths. These are line, shape, form, colour, tone, pattern and texture. Whilst very young children have no need to specifically identify these elements, they provide a useful framework for thinking about the provision of resources and how to extend children's mathematical learning in creative ways.

- Generally the visual elements do not act in isolation but work well with each other. For example, laying out a pattern of cones and stones in a line covers the visual elements of pattern, colour, line and texture.

- Use inspirational work by artists to create patterns using natural objects *in situ*. Look at the following websites for year-round ideas:

  - Chris Drury: http://chrisdrury.co.uk/
  - Andy Goldsworthy: www.goldsworthy.cc.gla.ac.uk/
  - Marc Pouyet (in French): www.marc-pouyet.net/
  - Richard Schilling: http://richardshilling.co.uk/
  - Land Art for Kids: http://landartforkids.com/
  - Responsible Fishing (sculptures and stone work): www.responsiblefishinguk.co.uk/

Idea 8.19 Creating beautiful temporary patterns

Decorate features outside with found objects placed in repeating patterns – for example, stick clay or mud in rings around trees and push daisies and other flowers into the clay to make them stay. Tie cones onto fences in line with the fence chain pattern. Make interesting stick patterns around the edge of the playground – a quick form of decoration for an outdoor event or party.

Idea 8.20 Mazes and labyrinths

Mazes and labyrinths enable active explorations of pattern. Find out where the public ones are in your local area. A maze involves an element of problem-solving. It has dead ends, and working out how to negotiate these is part of the fun.

Labyrinths are for contemplating. They enable a person to walk further within a confined space and are created to support reflection through walking. The design of a labyrinth requires mathematical knowledge and precision when measuring it out. It is usually created using a grid pattern, examples of which can be found through a quick online search.

With very young children, it is the experience of mazes and labyrinths that often leads them on to wanting to design or create their own versions. Children are happy simply to invent their own small-scale mazes by making tracks and paths in sand, mud or other soft surfaces. Always ask for an explanation and demonstration of how their mazes or labyrinths work.

Idea 8.21 Line pattern explorations

Line patterns are closely linked to mark making (see Ideas 2.8 and 2.9). They elicit a practical exploration of rules and physical attributes in many different ways. Encourage the children to describe the patterns made. Make lines and patterns with ropes of different lengths and sizes. Children like making zigzag waves and snakes by moving rope up and down or from side to side.

- Making interesting patterns with rope. Dip the rope in water and take it for a walk on a dry day.

- Provide ribbons on sticks for creating loops and spirals. On Bonfire night, children can be carefully supervised as they create similar patterns with sparklers.

- Make patterns of long continuous lines of objects. Provide natural objects with which the children can make trails. This can fit into many themes – for example, pirates finding treasure, following big footprints to find a hidden dinosaur, Spiderman leaving a trail of silk to where he has captured a villain.

Idea 8.22 Masking tape line art

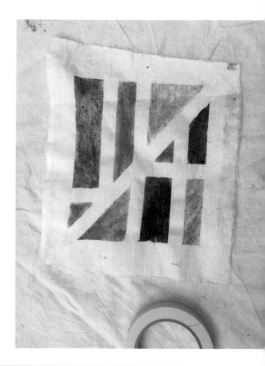

Stick masking tape to small squares of plain, old sheeting. The cotton squares are then rubbed with mud, berries, plant leaves and other found items. Do a check of the outside area beforehand to ensure nothing unsuitable will be collected and rubbed. Eventually the areas of sheet not covered by masking tape will be a range of colours. When the masking tape is removed, very clear line patterns emerge, as well as a range of shapes which provide a good basis for mathematical discussions.

Children enjoy being able to make lines and patterns outside by freely sticking masking tape to different features and creating long lines.[3] This does use up a lot of masking tape, however. When gathering up the tape afterwards, squash it into clumps so that it can be used for dipping in paint and printing with the following day.

---

3 This blog post provides a useful starting point into line investigations with masking tape: J. Robertson, More masking tape, *Creative Star Learning* (16 March 2011). Available at: http://creativestarlearning.co.uk/early-years-outdoors/more-masking-tape/.

Idea 8.23 Lines in the real world

What lines can the children find outside and what is their purpose? This can make a good topic of conversation on a walk if a child notices an interesting pattern of lines. Think about power lines, washing lines, road markings, playground markings, lines of fence posts or lamp posts and so on.

Do straight lines exist in nature? If so, what examples can be found? Spiders' webs are best seen on dewy mornings. Remember to look closely at plants as well as animals.

Idea 8.24 Strategy and logic games

Strategy and logic games can be found in all countries and cultures. Many are well suited to being played outside using found objects. All the games involve looking for patterns and knowing the cause and effect of moves undertaken in particular sequences. This usually involves playing the game lots of times and experimenting with different moves. Some basic points include:

- Children need time to learn each game by just enjoying the experience of playing it. Older children or adult volunteers can assist here. Hold a games session so that parents and carers can learn different games too.

- Encourage the children to make a board game – it is challenging and fun. Chalk can be used, as can sticks or lines drawn in sand, grit, mud or other soft surfaces.

- If a game isn't going well, ask the children for their ideas about making it better. What rules could be adapted or changed? How can they make the game more exciting?

- Games can be adapted to help the children acquire specific skills in many areas of maths. When you do this, it can be helpful to seek the children's thoughts and suggestions. This gives them ownership of their learning and facilitates a personal interest.

- Teach some games that the children can play on their own. Show them how to use soft toys to play a game, so that they are the referees and control the decision-making of the soft toys!

- Once the children are proficient at playing a game, then start asking questions which help to develop their strategic thinking. For example:

  - Does it matter who goes first?

  - How do you make sure you win?

  - What would happen if …?

The NRICH website has lots of advice and examples of strategy games, including a specific early years section with many play-based suggestions.[4] The maths section of my Creative STAR website has lots of examples of logic and strategy games, along with open-ended investigations which work well outside.[5]

Idea 8.25 Noughts and crosses

This is a simple game that young children can easily master. The grid can be made from sticks. Once a child becomes proficient, it is worth asking about the strategies they use to ensure a win and how they avoid a draw. The game can be extended by:

- Increasing the size of the grid. What happens when the game is played on a 4 x 4 grid?

- Increasing the size of the grid and the number of players. What happens when three people play the game?

- Increasing the size of the grid *and* the winner has to achieve a straight line of four in a row.

Idea 8.26 Grid patterns

The grids on which many strategy games are played are worthy of investigation. For example, if you have a 3 x 3 grid, how many different patterns can you create by placing five stones within this grid? This is surprisingly complex as it raises discussions about what constitutes a unique pattern. Adults can model how to record the different patterns through taking photos or noting down the patterns on paper.

---

4 See: https://nrich.maths.org/early-years.
5 See: http://creativestarlearning.co.uk/c/maths-outdoors/.

Idea 8.27 White line pebbles

White line pebbles are a set of flat stones which have white lines painted on them.[6] They can be used for open-ended investigative pattern work. Develop a large collection so that many children can join in or so big patterns can be created. The investigations can be undertaken step by step.

- Begin with single white lines. Observe and record what patterns the children make.

- Introduce right-angle white line pebbles. Observe and record how this changes the patterns the children make.

- Show the children other white line pebble patterns such as Y shapes, T bars and V forks. Ask them which they would like to use.

- Encourage the children to design their own pebbles to add to the collection.

- Look at other forms of white lines such as curly squiggles.

Idea 8.28 Rainbow maths sticks

Rainbow maths sticks are sticks which have the ends painted different colours. They are an open-ended resource that encourages children to investigate patterns through their own play and by designing their own games. They can be informal collections created by the children, simply by collecting sticks and dipping each end in paint.

It is also possible to create specific sets that facilitate different types of pattern making and investigative play. These can be made in different ways, such as painting sticks with a suitable waterproof paint or wrapping electrical tape around each end. Have lots of sticks available so that a group of children can explore. For example:

- Provide sets with only two colours.

- Have a range of colours but each stick should have the same colour at both ends.

- Create a colour set based on the domino system.[7]

---

6 For more on this see: J. Robertson, White line pebble maths, *Creative Star Learning* (12 July 2014). Available at: http://creativestarlearning.co.uk/art-music-outdoors/white-line-pebble-maths/.

7 This blog post provides comprehensive instructions and suggestions: J. Robertson, Rainbow maths sticks, *Creative Star Learning* (8 April 2014). Available at: http://creativestarlearning.co.uk/maths-outdoors/rainbow-maths-sticks/.

When I observe children making or investigating patterns with rainbow sticks, I ask questions such as:

■ Have you invented any games which use the sticks, and if so, what are the rules?

■ What is the outcome when you make a change to the rule?

■ Does any colour of stick have a special power? What would happen in your game if you added a new different coloured stick?

■ Have you added any plain sticks into the game or any other objects?

In addition to children developing their own games, rainbow sticks work well when used to:

■ Play line-up. Can the children order the sticks logically?

■ Play odd one out. If one stick is removed from a given set, can a child work out which one is missing?

■ Play the traditional dominoes game – the lines of sticks bring variety.

■ Explore numbers. The colours can each be given a value (e.g. red = 1, orange = 2, yellow = 3). How would this change the game that is played? For example, when two colours are placed together, what would the total be?

■ Play pick-up sticks. Create a pile of sticks and then take turns to remove one stick without disturbing any others. If other sticks are moved, then the turn passes to the next player. Does placing a value on the colour of the sticks add to or detract from the level of strategy involved?

CHAPTER 9

Shape and Symmetry

Investigating and exploring shape and space is an inherent part of children's mathematical development. If you observe young children playing freely in an outdoor environment, their ability to navigate obstacles, lift, move and stack objects or push and pull items are all examples of experiences of geometry that come naturally to them. Without the time to explore spaces and shapes in all their forms, it becomes harder for children to develop the intuition, imagination and spatial awareness needed to understand the key concepts which underpin this aspect of maths.

Outside, the range of standard and non-standard shapes and variety of uniform and non-uniform spaces is extraordinary. It is a place to learn in practical ways. For example:

- Investigating holes and posting things into them.

- Discovering the range of shapes that exist in different environments, especially being able to compare man-made and natural spaces and the patterns that shapes create.

- Exploring the different properties of shapes and how these help us to move shapes about or use them for different purposes.

- Learning about space through moving in, out, up, down and around structures – vertically and horizontally.

- Creating two-dimensional images and three-dimensional models and taking them apart.

- Using sand, snow, mud and clay to sculpt, manipulate and flatten shapes.

- Finding the relationship between two- and three-dimensional shapes through drawing around, printing and making pictures with them.

- Learning the associated vocabulary and concepts, supported by practitioners who can explain and demonstrate ideas to stretch the children's thinking.

Those children who struggle with number work often find they can identify with shape and spatial awareness. It is a form of mathematical thinking which involves feeling, moving and physically exploring with the whole body.

Generally, it is expected that children will learn:

- To recognise common two-dimensional shapes and three-dimensional objects.

- To identify the properties of shapes – such as, the number of vertices, straight and curved sides, straight and curved edges, flat and curved faces, and whether they can roll, slide, be stacked or packed or fit well together.

- How shapes are classified and to be able to sort them according to their attributes, considering what is the same (equivalence) and what is different (transformation).

- That shapes can change. They can be transformed in different ways. They may also look different when viewed from a range of perspectives.

- To use vocabulary associated with shape and space.

It's all about equivalence and transformation

Derek Haylock and Anne Cockburn state the need for teachers to 'recognise the significance and value of informal and intuitive experience of shape and spatial concepts through play and other activities in and out of the classroom'.[1] They also state that the concepts of equivalence and transformation are fundamental not just to understanding number but also shape. At its most simple, this is about considering what is the same and what is different.

It was a light bulb moment for me when the link between children's explorations of their environment and the types of transformation that can be applied to shapes became apparent. Haylock and Cockburn enabled me to understand that children need a much broader experience of shape beyond playing with collections of traditional shapes and objects. It is about the play-based groundwork being laid for later exploration and deeper understanding of geometrical concepts.

Haylock and Cockburn consider the types of transformation in order of increasing distortion of the original shape: translation, rotation, reflection, similarity, affinity (family likeness), perspectivity and topological transformation. This can be explained in the context of outdoor play as follows:

1   Translation. We can observe translation in children's play when objects are being moved to a different place. It is sliding a shape or object vertically, horizontally or diagonally. This represents the beginnings of work on direction and concepts such as up, down, left, right, forwards and backwards. Pulley systems (see Idea 6.17) allow items to be translated across a space both vertically and horizontally.

2   Rotation. When a shape or object is turned clockwise or anticlockwise. By rotating objects, and themselves, children learn the foundations of rotational symmetry (see Idea 9.14).

---

1   Haylock and Cockburn, *Understanding Mathematics for Young Children*, p. 259.

3   Reflection. When a shape or object is flipped over a mirror line. This is considered in more detail in the work on symmetry later in this chapter.

4   Similarity. With this transformation, the size, area or volume of the shape or object may change. For example, when scaling a shape and making it larger or smaller, the edges increase or decrease in length by uniform amounts but the angles remain unchanged. Thus nesting crates which fit inside each other are an example of similarity.

5   Affinity (family likeness). When the length of the sides of shapes change, with or without a change in position or movement, this is referred to as family likeness. This can often confuse children who, without a lot of practical experience of making, using and discussing triangles in their play, may have trouble recognising that an isosceles triangle and an equilateral triangle are both triangles.

6   Perspectivity. This is about learning to recognise a shape or object when viewed from different perspectives (see Idea 9.12). However, it also includes experiences such as climbing trees and viewing known places from a height, or looking out of a den, hedge or enclosed space. Views of the landscape can also help because of the feeling of space and size that results.

7   Topological transformation. This is the most distorting of all transformations. When children use clay, they will pull, stretch and distort its original form in lots of different ways. Likewise, a two-dimensional shape can be distorted as long as no lines are broken or joined in the process. For instance, an elastic band can be stretched and manipulated to create a range of shapes that look very different from its original form. Topological work is also experienced by children when they are:

○   Learning to read different fonts.

○   Being given a set of directions to get from one place to another – it is unlikely that even an adult will refer to scale or distance.

○   Playing position and movement games which rely on instructions such as 'near to', 'in-between' or 'beside'.

○   Creating maps and miniature worlds, such as shaping a fixed amount of sand.

○   Playing with ropes and other long materials which remain intact.

The explorations of networks, paths, journeys and movement described in Chapter 10 are connected to work on shape and topological transformations.

Think before you speak …

It is more important that children have lots of practical experiences of playing with shapes, rather than worrying about them knowing the mathematical names for lots of different shapes. Try not to ruin deep mathematical play by interrupting to talk about vertices and the difference between a pyramid and a prism when the children are exploring and having fun.

There is ongoing debate amongst educators about what certain shapes should be called according to their properties. For example, all squares are rectangles but not all rectangles are squares. Some maths experts prefer to use the terms 'oblong rectangle' and 'square rectangle' to distinguish between the two types. It can be helpful to agree terminology within your team or school to ensure there is consistency of use.

Vocabulary

Above, angle, anticlockwise, backwards, behind, below, between, circle, clockwise, closer, coordinates, cone, cube, cuboid, curved, down, drawing, edge, face, far, flat, forwards, further, here, hexagon, higher, in front of, inside, junction, left, line symmetry, long, lower, map, mirror line, near, network, next, oblong rectangle, opposite, outside, oval, path, pentagon, plan, position, prism, quadrilateral, region, regular sides, rhombus, right, right angle, roll, scale, short, side, similar, slide, smooth, solid, sphere, square rectangle, stack, straight, there, triangle, up

Expressions

The shape of things to come

Shaping the future

Having square eyes

Trying to fit a square peg into a round hole

Introducing two-dimensional shapes and three-dimensional objects

For me, children's experiences of two-dimensional shapes and three-dimensional objects go hand in hand. We live in a three-dimensional world: toys and other objects are predominantly three-dimensional by their nature. Yet children are more likely to recognise two-dimensional shapes first, such as referring to wheels on a car as 'circles'. It is hard not to discuss plane (flat) shapes as these can be seen on the surface of every solid object.

Idea 9.1 Three-dimensional shape dens

Lash together wooden poles or long broom handles to create large dens in the style of cubes, cuboids and square-based and triangular pyramids. Have a range of different fabrics available so the children can adapt them and make them their own. Which is the most popular shape and why? Which shape fits the largest number of children inside?

Idea 9.2 Hiding objects to be discovered

Children develop a sense of shape and space by hiding objects and finding them again. The children can hide objects in the sand area, under stones or behind logs for others to find. Have some containers ready for sorting the finds.

Outside, you can provide lots of old bags and large and small boxes so the children can hide toys and collectables. You don't need to buy special sets; instead go for things which fit inside each other. For example, put a shell inside a little box. Put the little box inside a small bag. Put the small bag inside a big bag. Hang this up outside and wait for the children to discover the present within!

Idea 9.3 Viewing frames

Viewing frames help children to focus when observing the world. They also help to build their understanding of similarity when using and comparing frames of different sizes but similar shapes. They can be taken on walks or used as windows during den building. Consider a variety of:

■ Two-dimensional shapes. These can be pre-cut from cereal boxes or card. Does the shape of the viewer affect what can be seen?

■ Three-dimensional shapes. Telescopes and binoculars are examples of three-dimensional viewers. Many young children enjoy decorating toilet tubes and the triangular prisms that house Swiss chocolate. Does the length or width of the viewer impact on its effectiveness?

■ Sizes. Have a range of frames from small to large. Create sets which fit inside each other for added interest and value.

■ Viewers with flaps. This works well for babies and toddlers who love playing peek-a-boo. If you attach an acrylic mirror, the children can enjoy looking at their own reflection as well as looking at the world behind them with the mirror.

■ Leaves. Hole punches work well for creating little circles in leaves. These are nature spyglasses. They are helpful for spies and detectives who can quickly hide behind them to avoid being discovered!

Idea 9.4 Stick shape frames

Use strong straight sticks and string to make two-dimensional natural frames. It is particularly effective if the children cut the sticks themselves. These can be used in a multitude of ways to help children consolidate the names and properties of different shapes.

■ Use the frames when den building. Children often choose to use them as windows.

- The children could wrap scrap wool and lengths of material around them in a range of patterns.

- Add twine or string to create natural weaving frames.

- Mobiles. Hang them vertically or horizontally and attach objects. For example, every child could find a natural object when on a walk or at a greenspace and hang it from a shape frame as a memory of the experience.

- Shape pictures. Use the shape frame to create a character. Which part of the body would the shape frame become? Also make chalk or a choice of natural materials available for decoration.

- Frames can make seasonal decorations such as stars for Christmas trees – just attach one triangle upside down on top of another triangle.

- With bigger sticks, make frames that the children can go behind to pose for portrait photos (great fun after the school photographer has visited).

- By altering the lengths of the sticks used, the concept of family likeness can be explored informally.

Idea 9.5 Shape hunting

When walking out and about, children enjoy observing and commenting on their surroundings as part of their discussions.

- Which shapes do the children like the best?

- Which are interesting shapes?

- Do any shapes remind them of something else?

- Why does an object have the particular shape it does?

- Is it possible to find regular shapes, such as squares or circles, in natural features and objects?

As the children's knowledge and understanding of shapes develops you can provide sheets or cards with simple drawings of different shapes and their names. Remember to include three-dimensional objects and simple tessellations. The children may wish to take photos of the shapes they find in nature. They could create a book about shapes in the environment based around the photos. This will involve a lot of decision-making about how to categorise their findings.

Idea 9.6 | Holes

Holes are pockets of space and can be artificial or natural constructs (see also Idea 13.4). When children dig holes they become creators of space. Observe the maths involved. For example, the children may try to cover a hole with their hands to see if this will stop objects passing in or out, demonstrating a form of non-standard measurement. They may choose to put their arm inside a hole, checking its diameter as they do so.

If you provide a range of loose parts, such as cones, sticks, stones and shells, the children will explore what resources can fit into a hole, thus developing their understanding of the size of one object in relation to another. When a child decides to fill up a hole with objects, or materials such as sand or water, then their understanding of volume and capacity is developing. When a hole is emptied, this is the equivalent of subtracting volume.

Adults can also consider the mathematical play value of holes when setting up different areas in an outdoor space. The range of possible holes is huge.

■ Tubes are effectively long holes. You can also cut holes into tubes such as guttering to add interest to water play. This will affect the volume of water and the speed at which it passes down a water wall.

■ Hoses are also long holes. Use these for communicating through and for playing with loose materials such as water, sand and gravel.

■ Look for holes in loose parts. Children enjoy posting material through the holes in milk and bread crates. Tyres are also holey.

Holes bridge the gap between the man-made and natural world. Children are fascinated by natural holes in tree stumps and trunks, rabbit and other animal holes and the development of tunnels, which are essentially elongated holes. Hollow stems are another example of holes. Features of animals such as pelicans' beaks and kangaroos' pouches add further interest.

Idea 9.7 Shape shifting

Finding out how many children can fit onto, inside or around objects lends itself to any outdoor space and any impromptu moment. For example:

■ How many children can stand on a tree stump without falling off?

■ How many children could sit on a picnic rug and still have space to eat their snack?

■ Does the length of a piece of rope affect the number of children who can stand inside a shape made by that rope?

■ What is the smallest shape that can be chalked on the ground for two children to stand in?

■ What is the quickest shape or set of shapes that can be drawn by a class that everyone can stand in? This is a very interesting challenge as it is open to interpretation.

Idea 9.8 Making a music area from shapes

Many noisy objects have interesting shapes. Use dustbin lids, pan lids, old triangles from the music cupboard, long rectangle-shaped chime bars, cylindrical wind chimes, tins of different sizes and so on. Hang these from a tree or branch or attach to a fence outside. Encourage the children to sort and hang the objects according to their shape. Provide plenty of opportunity to explore the impact of the attributes (e.g. shape, composite material, size) on the sound that can be heard.

Exploring properties of shapes

Idea **9.9** Stacking

Stacking is a key property of some three-dimensional objects. Outside, children may enjoy stacking the following objects:

- Milk crates, bread crates, tyres and fish boxes. How will a child be supported once they try to stack these beyond their own height?

- Cardboard boxes. Children sometimes enjoy the challenge of trying to add a box to a tall stack that is beyond their reach through the use of a high pulley system.

- Stones or bricks – for creating walls. This sort of project is particularly worthwhile in spaces where the work can be left for the children to continue over a series of days or weeks.

- Alternatively, gather a collection of different three-dimensional objects and leave in the construction zone. Observe the children's choice of objects for stacking.

Idea 9.10 | Shell stacks and other miniature challenges

Lots of objects lend themselves to miniature stacking and balancing challenges. Shells can be a good starting point when visiting a beach as they are generally easier to stack than stones. They can also be used to create curved structures such as bridges.

Other miniature stacking challenges include:

- Wooden discs. Offcuts of unfinished wood are ideal, whilst wood cookies work well for babies and children who are developing their coordination.

- Stones. Use flat stones for this purpose. To increase the level of challenge, have a collection from which children need to pick out the flat stones to make them stack.

- Beechnut husks. These can be gently pushed one on top of the other as they are slightly spiky. If this is too hard then go for a horizontal stack!

- What is the biggest shell stack a child can make without adult input? Have this as an ongoing record.

Idea 9.11 | Simple stacking challenges

Stacking challenges do not need to be formal teaching moments. Instead, it is better to have a list to hand so that should children need a challenge you have one ready to go or that can be adapted. You can encourage children to come up with their own challenges too. Here are some suggestions:

- The highest tower you can possibly build.

- A stack as tall as a friend.

- A stone stack with more than three stones.

- A castle that uses all the blocks.

- A house with the bricks laid in the same pattern as a real house.

- A fairy tower using wooden noggins.

- A set of steps that can be walked up and down.

This is also a good opportunity to help the children to make connections between maths and technology or construction activities. These tasks can be linked through role play to the children's interests, such as being on a building site.

When discussing children's stacking and constructions, adults can:

- Refer to the faces they see.
- Talk about curved and straight edges.
- Count the number of vertices/corners.
- Discuss which shapes are easiest to stack and why.
- Consider which are the most robust constructions and why.
- Wonder whether it is possible to move a stack of objects and consider the best ways of doing this.
- Provide the mathematical names of different shapes.

Idea 9.12 Building models

There are many large-scale construction kits which are designed for use outside. Often they come with illustrations for building specific items. Some kits come with a miniature or table-top version for helping children to plan their designs.

Many children have interests which can also be channelled into model making. For example, a child who is fascinated with fire engines may choose to look at a photo or picture of a fire engine in a book as a guide to creating their interpretation of one in three-dimensional form outside using any available natural or man-made materials. The need to make do with what they have and can find adds an extra dimension of critical thinking.

Building models and constructions is also a useful context for children to learn about perspective. You can encourage them to systematically take photos of their three-dimensional models from all sides, including above and even below if this is possible. Likewise, a child who enjoys sketching and drawing can also do this from different angles.

Idea 9.13 Taking models apart and putting them back together again

The process of deconstruction can be as simple as learning to take down a shelter and then put it back up again. Sometimes it is easier to begin with taking something down or apart so that we can remember what we want it to look like. Always take photos or a video before deconstruction as a reference point!

Cardboard boxes are a surprisingly tricky deconstruction challenge. If possible, obtain pairs of boxes so that one can stay stuck together whilst the other is deconstructed into its net. Highlight different parts of the box with different coloured permanent marker pens to draw attention to the names of the different parts of the box (e.g. edge, face/surface, vertices).

Idea 9.14 | Introducing rotation

Rotation begins with children physically experiencing the turning of shapes, objects and also themselves. This lends itself to outdoor explorations. For example:

- Turning a door knob to get outside.

- Swinging gates and doors backwards and forwards (the rotation happens on the hinge).

- Swinging on swings, especially rope swings which enable children to spin around as well as swing backwards and forwards.

- Playing with playground equipment which involves rotating or turning.

- Learning to use a screw and screwdriver and attach nuts and bolts.

- Rolling down a hill (how many times does a child rotate between two points?).

- Spinning on the spot.

- Learning how to hula hoop.

- Spinning little and large objects – such as hula hoops, spinners, balls and coins.

- Watching sycamore seeds helicopter to the ground.

- Practising position and movement activities linked to turns.

- Playing games and singing action songs which involve rotation, either by individual children or as a group, such as moving round as a circle.

- Moving resources – for example, a play house may be carried across the play space and then turned to face a different direction.

Idea 9.15 Link rotation to shapes through drawing

Children can explore how rotation is linked to shapes through drawing around moveable objects outside. Provide chalk and big objects like tyres or crates for the children to draw around. Encourage accuracy but remember this is a skill that takes time to develop. Talk about the size of the objects and how much space they take up on the ground. For younger children, this can be done more easily outdoors in the sand or gravel area using a stick or their finger.

If a child chalks the outline of a milk crate, they can see how many different ways the crate will fit into the outline without turning it over. A circle or the circular face of a cylinder (e.g. a pipe) will have infinite ways of fitting into its outline. Remember to comment on whether a rotation is clockwise or anticlockwise when you see a child do this.

Idea 9.16 Posting shapes

Get the children to post shapes through holes which match the outline of the shape. For example, a cross will fit into a cross hole in four different ways, whereas an oval shape will fit through in only one of two possible ways, providing the shape is only rotated and not flipped over.

By introducing vocabulary such as 'quarter turn' and 'half a turn', the language of fractions is being used. Half and quarter turns are the starting points for linking angles to rotation. A dynamic angle is the measure of the amount of turn or rotation which has occurred. A quarter turn is a right angle or a rotation of 90 degrees.

Idea 9.17 Flat dens

This idea follows on from drawing around three-dimensional objects. Children use two-dimensional shape outlines on the ground to create 'maps' on asphalt. For example, the children may enjoy drawing a house where they can 'live', where a rectangle might become a bed and three squares might become the kitchen.

Objects can be used to represent different features too: a rope can be used to outline a house, a pallet can become a bed, a box can be the cooker and so on.

Idea 9.18 Matching a real object to a photo

Children can create their own scavenger hunt challenges by taking photos of things they see in their outdoor space using a digital device such as a tablet. The group then has to go and find each object in turn and stand beside it. Alternatively, once the children have brought an item to a gathering circle, they can take a photo of it. Once everyone has taken a photo, a slide show can happen and the children take turns to point to or hold up the object in the photo. By matching objects to photos, the connection between solid objects and two-dimensional images is being consolidated.

Idea 9.19 Shape describing games

In conjunction with your group or class of children, invent games which involve describing the properties of different shapes and objects. It is always helpful to have the shapes available so the children have a visual cue to associate with the description being heard. As children's descriptions often lack precision to begin with, an adult can ask questions to introduce and model vocabulary. Possibilities include:

- Using a feely bag to describe a shape based on touch.

- Giving a description of a shape that can be found in the environment.

- Having shapes marked on the ground to go and stand in, if working with a large class of children.

- The shape magician: hide one shape in a pocket or up a sleeve and slowly reveal it until someone can guess what shape it is.

Idea 9.20 What's the rule?

For this game you need a collection of shapes, numbers or objects. Begin to sort these into two sets – for example:

- Fewer than four petals and more than four petals.
- Yellow and not yellow.
- Four-sided shapes and not four-sided shapes.

The aim is for the other players to guess the rule by suggesting additional items. It also gives the children opportunities to develop their vocabulary of shape and space and to focus on equivalences. It can be played outside using examples found in nature, picked up objects, number pebbles and so on.

Other challenges that can build upon this include:

- Finding an object in the environment which matches a shape in a set.
- Copying and recreating two-dimensional shapes from a set using sticks.
- Using puppets and making up a little story about why the items need to be sorted.

Idea 9.21 Change one stick

Ask each child to find and bring a stick to a gathering circle. In turn, the children contribute towards creating a group picture as they add their stick to the white sheet. Once the picture is complete, discuss the different shapes seen. Use the opportunity to talk about straight and curved sides, vertices, and the need for the sticks to be touching each other because two-dimensional shapes do not have gaps, otherwise they are just lines.

Next, each child in turn may move one stick and put it elsewhere in the picture. The children will comment on the changing picture. You may wish to take photos after each turn so they can keep track of the changes. Upload the photos into an animation app and the children will be able to see the changes taking place.

Idea 9.22 Creating shapes

■ Is it possible to make a shape using only three sticks? Ask each child to pick three straight sticks and make a shape, ensuring each stick is touching the others. See what patterns each child produces.

■ Show the children a triangle and ask them to copy it using their sticks. Next, ask each of them to take one stick and swap it with another person's. Ask the children to notice what happens when the length of one of the sticks is changed.

■ Then they should have a go at making another triangle. Discuss whether the triangles look the same as or different to before. Encourage the children to show their triangles and discuss the similarities and differences between them.

■ Challenge the children to make a triangle that is different to the one they have just made using another three sticks.

■ What happens when a fourth stick is introduced? How does this affect the shapes which are made?

This activity can be repeated for other shapes such as squares and rectangles. Use short lengths of rope, such as skipping ropes or one metre ropes, to make ovals and circles.

Idea 9.23 Two-dimensional stick pictures

Using twelve straight sticks, challenge the children to make an interesting shape picture. They can work by themselves or with a partner. Once they have done this, follow up with other challenges, such as:

■ Ask them to show you different two-dimensional shapes which appear in their pictures. For example, can they show you a triangle? Which is the largest rectangle? Which shape has the most vertices?

■ Can they recreate the shape only using small sticks? What happens to the picture? What happens if a range of stick lengths is used? Does the picture become distorted?

My sticks aren't straight enough – they don't make perfect shapes

I find working outside can help me to think more flexibly about maths. When we make a shape with sticks we are creating an *approximate representation* of an abstract mathematical idea. In my experience, most children will readily accept a gentle bend in a stick and understand that it is being used to illustrate the side of a shape. Likewise, the vertices of shapes are represented where two sticks meet.

Technically, two-dimensional shapes only exist pictorially as even the thinnest of them has height as well as area, so even standard bought two-dimensional shapes are approximate representations. Equally, there is no such thing as a perfect right angle or a precise one metre length.

Exploring printing

Using three-dimensional objects for printing activities which enable the children to see the printed surface can help to develop their understanding of the objects' properties. Generally, flat faces produce prints that mirror the face and curved faces do not. Try out some different types of printing, as outlined below.

Idea 9.24 Water imprints

By placing objects or shapes on the ground and then spraying or pouring water over them, the children can make the connection between a three-dimensional object and its associated two-dimensional shape. A good variation on this theme is to leave a few toys out when it begins to rain. After a few minutes, let the children lift up the toys and see the silhouette left behind.

Idea 9.25 Paint dipping

Dip three-dimensional objects in paint or runny mud and roll them over a piece of paper or a sheet on the ground. Sometimes curved surfaces look very different – for example, if the children roll a cone, what shape is made on the ground? Let the children dip spheres of different sizes, textures and weights – from tiny marbles to big footballs – into paint or water and roll them across asphalt. This can create some rather fetching patterns.

Idea 9.26 Body printing

When out on a walk, children enjoy seeing their footprints left in a variety of surfaces: grass, snow, sand and mud. Get the children to jump and observe both footprints beside each other so they can see the symmetrical shape made. A natural complement to this activity is to press hard objects into soft surfaces, then lift them up and see what pattern they have made.

The class can dip their hands into paint, mud or wet clay and place their handprints onto an old sheet. The children can also go barefoot over the ground and create footprints on sheets placed outside. It can be fun to compare a foot dipped in paint with the footprint that has been created. What other parts of their bodies can be used for printing?

Idea 9.27 Large scale printing

Use a big sheet and hang it up against a wall or pin it to the ground. Print with big items, such as:

- Balls dipped in paint and bounced off the ground. This will create discussion – why is the print a splat and not a circle?

- Sticks – these are great for looking at lines and creating line patterns.

- Bread and milk crates.

- Wheels from bikes, trikes or scooters.

Idea 9.28 Three-dimensional snow shapes

Snow is a wonderful medium for any shape work, especially on a large scale. Challenge the children to build:

- The largest snowball – a snow sphere.

- A snow monster – think about the shapes of the scales and other parts of its body.

- Forts and rooms that are interesting shapes.

- Three-dimensional models by packing snow into containers and then gently emptying them out, similar to building sandcastles.

Idea 9.29 | Introducing the concept of scale

Scale is a transformation that is classified as a similarity. The difference is that the size of a shape is affected by a specific factor, such as twice as large or one-tenth of the size. Informally, children will encounter scale through:

- Small world play items.

- Different sorts of maps and being able to zoom in and out when using digital maps, Google Earth and similar apps.

- Noticing features which are significantly bigger. Remember that scale is about increasing and decreasing the size of an object.

- The use of magnifying glasses of different scales.

- Playing with large and small sticks of specific sizes, such as 50 cm and 25 cm lengths.

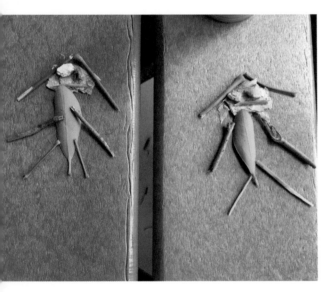

Symmetry

Symmetry is a beautiful and artistic aspect of space and shape in which objects are reflected and rotated. Reflective symmetry involves a translation along a mirror line and also the flipping over of a shape. A good way to demonstrate this is to open a book placed horizontally on a flat surface. Rotational symmetry is just what it says on the packet: it is the number of times an object will fit into its own shape when rotated around a central point.

Children need support to identify, recognise and articulate symmetry observed in natural and man-made surroundings. Symmetry begins with reflections and mirror images, particularly those associated with their own bodies, such as looking in a mirror or an awareness that they have hands, arms, legs and feet that are mirror images of each other. As children's understanding develops, so their ability to recognise and create their own symmetrical patterns improves.

Tiling is another entry point into symmetry. Take time when on walks and out and about in urban areas to enjoy examples of tiling and the symmetry which can be observed. Take mirrors with you to explore this in more detail.

Idea 9.30 Exploring reflections

The outside world is full of reflective surfaces waiting to be discovered.

- Go for a reflective walk and find window panes, puddles, stretches of calm water, mirrors on cars, reflective sculptures and shiny surfaces such as car doors.

- Deploy small acrylic mirrors in different colours and shapes for general exploration outdoors. You can use them as a mark-making surface too. Add them to wheeled vehicles so the children can look behind them.

- Use distorting reflective objects and ask the children to observe what they see and how their size and shape changes. Distorting mirrors include concave and convex examples such as spoons and Christmas baubles. Unwanted CDs can be used to create rainbows and distorted images.

- Kaleidoscopes and periscopes are portable resources for general explorations.

- Create a shallow pool of water for examining reflections. Can the children see the sky in the water? What about their faces? What happens when a stone is dropped into the water?

- Two mirrors taped together enable children to experiment further with reflections. Are the images accurate reflections, or does distortion begin to happen when two or more mirrors are used?

- Use reflective discs and clothes with integral reflective strips, such as high visibility tabards. Discuss why reflective material is used in jackets, trainers and other outdoor clothes and how this differs to mirror reflections. Is this ability to reflect light the same as a mirror's ability to reflect an image?

Be mindful that some reflective material can create litter outside, so encourage vigilance about keeping an eye out for inadvertent littering and picking up rubbish to avoid harm to wildlife. Store mirrors out of direct sunlight as a fire safety precaution.

Idea 9.31 How to reflect light off a mirror safely

This involves catching the sun on a mirror and directing the light onto the ground, a wall or elsewhere. Have fun following the light pattern created outside. Coloured mirrors provide different colours to follow. You will need to model this activity and show the children how to do this without looking at the sun's rays. The children will also need to know that they should never reflect the sun into or near another person's eyes.

Idea 9.32 Mirror image games

When children are facing a mirror, call out instructions from behind and the children can watch themselves carry these out. They will have lots of good ideas for moving too. Next, extend this game into children copying an adult or another child's actions as if they are their mirror.

Follow my leader is also a form of reflective movement. It is an interesting thing to do occasionally when on walks. Whoever is at the front of the line performs simple actions for the others behind to copy. This might be lifting one arm in the air, doing a series of jumps, walking sideways or other ideas the children come up with.

The detective game is an extension of follow my leader. The group sits in a circle. One person is chosen to be the detective, who leaves the circle. The rest of the group decide who will be the leader. The group call back the detective, who stands in the middle of the circle. The leader starts making an action, such as pretending to brush their hair, and everyone in the group copies the action. The leader can change the action whenever they wish. The detective has to work out who is the leader. Once this happens, a new leader and detective are chosen.

Idea 9.33 Does symmetry exist in nature?

Whilst perfect symmetry is quite challenging to find, approximate representations are much easier to discover. A mirror can be useful for checking – model how to do this for the children. Some leaf species such as beech (*Fagus sylvatica*) can be folded down the midrib, which is another way of checking how symmetrical a leaf may be. Is it possible to find two leaves which are exactly the same?

Idea 9.34 Introducing the mirror line

Butterflies and butterfly painting lend themselves naturally to the idea of lines of symmetry and are traditional ways of introducing the concept to young children. Ladybirds and many other beetles also have a natural line of symmetry down their backs. This is called bilateral symmetry. Humans and other animals have bilateral symmetry for the purposes of movement. However, do remember that many of our internal organs are asymmetric (e.g. we only have one heart).

Idea 9.35 Hapa-zome

Hapa-zome is a Japanese printing technique which involves placing freshly picked plants between two sheets of cotton. The fabric is then pounded with a hammer, mallet or stone. When the plant matter is removed, the colour is left on the material. This can then be dried and hung up like bunting or framed as a present. It is a good use of garden weeds.

Idea 9.36 Find five

A simple symmetry game involves one child placing five objects found outside down one side of a line. Their partner or an adult must find objects to match and place them in a symmetrical way on the other side of the line, so that the object on one side reflects the same object on the other side.

Idea 9.37 Cardboard cut-outs

Cardboard cut-outs of butterflies, beetles and other symmetrical animals can be used for creating simple symmetrical patterns. Make clay available so the children can stick leaves, flower petals and other objects in symmetrical patterns on the cardboard silhouettes.

Once the children understand this, they can work with a partner to create symmetrical pattern pictures using found objects. As they develop their understanding of symmetry, the pictures can become increasingly complex.

Idea 9.38 Nature mandalas

A quick online search for nature mandalas will reveal many examples of rotational symmetry which have been created through arranging stones, sticks, shells, leaves, dandelions and other natural materials in beautiful circle patterns. These can be large scale and involve a whole group working together, miniature (no bigger than a scone-sized clay circle) or somewhere in-between. This activity can work well when older and younger children are paired up, and it links nicely to environmental artwork (see Idea 8.18).

Idea 9.39 Photo Booth distortions

iPads have a mirror line function in their Photo Booth app. This works best if the children stand in the same place and take an ordinary photo followed by one with the Photo Booth mirror function. Some of these can be printed off so the axis of symmetry can be highlighted and the photos compared. Adult support will be needed. Children also enjoy investigating other distortions which are available in Photo Booth. Make time to talk about their photos, the ideas behind the photos they took and how the distortion happened.

Idea 9.40 Helical symmetry

Helical symmetry is seen in springs, slinky toys, spirals and drill bits. It is essentially rotational symmetry with a translation along the axis of rotation. The children should just have fun using different toys and equipment that exhibit helical symmetry. No complicated explanations are needed!

Plants often exhibit symmetry in their growth. If you look down from above, you can see the leaves come out of the stem in a helical form. Archimedes' screws are used in some water play features to move water up a hill.

CHAPTER 10

Position, Direction and Movement

Position, direction and movement are aspects of maths which have clear links to physical play. As children grow, they become increasingly aware of what they can do with their bodies and the relationship their bodies have to objects around them. It's about developing and understanding spatial concepts.

Position is a relational concept and is about making connections between where a person or an object is in relation to other people or objects. Positional movement is about how a person or object moves and the direction of travel. It can include directions, way finding, journeys and routes.

In the earliest years, children enjoy walks with their parents, carers and key workers who, as part of everyday discussions, may introduce ideas such as how near or far away people and places are. They will witness scale at first hand when climbing steps and seeing the world looking increasingly smaller as they climb higher, or when being carried upon the shoulders of an adult and commanding a different viewpoint. Games such as hide-and-seek help to develop children's sense of perspective as they view the world from different angles and places. Likewise, hanging upside down is a fascination for many children, as is looking through their legs.

As children grow and develop, their ability to understand and use the vocabulary of position, direction and movement accurately will increase. From hearing and watching others model these words, they will move on to demonstrating their understanding through their ability to give and follow instructions and carry out tasks which require positional knowledge.

Directional concepts take longer to acquire. Remembering which is left and right, clockwise and anticlockwise, as well as the compass directions, is more abstract. The programming of some electronic toys requires an understanding of linking position to symbols (e.g. left = L). This jump to the abstract requires lots of meaningful work with concrete materials. In the early years, raising awareness is the aim in all these situations.

The geometric transformations outlined in Chapter 9 – translation, rotation, reflection, similarity, affinity (family likeness) and topological transformation – are inextricably linked to position, direction and movement.

Vocabulary

Above, anticlockwise, arrow, backwards, behind, below, beside, clockwise, close, compass, curved, direction, down, east, far, forwards, here, high, horizontal, in, in-between, in front of, inside, inside-out, left, line, low, near, next to, north, on top, out, outside, over, path, position, right, route, south, straight, there, through, turn, under, underneath, up, upside down, vertical, west

Expressions

Going round in circles

As straight as the crow flies

Bird's eye view

Topsy-turvy

Idea 10.1 Being specific with your use of positional language

Adults need to be specific rather than general in their use of positional and directional language. Much of the mathematical language can be modelled by adults commenting on what they see happening outside – for example, 'I saw you bounce *up* and *down on* the trampoline before you ran *across* the outdoor space to play with your friends *behind* the hedge.'

Adults can also share the delight of children who notice the position and movement of something beyond themselves. When children notice a lorry passing or a gull flying by, practitioners can use these opportunities to wonder aloud about relevant concepts – such as, 'I wonder where that lorry is going?' or 'How does that gull manage to swoop up and down so easily?' whilst making the gestures which indicate up and down.

Idea 10.2 Giving and following instructions and directions

Many routines by their very nature include directions and instructions which develop the understanding of position, direction and movement.

- Start with one-part directions such as, 'You need to get teddy *down* from the tree.'

- Move on to two-part directions and instructions: 'You need to get teddy *down* from the tree and put him *beside* rabbit.'

■ Get the children to tell others the instructions and give directions to help embed and aid understanding.

Idea 10.3   Run on ahead

Once children know the route and key landmarks on the way to a particular destination, the leader can give instructions such as, 'Do you see the big oak tree beside the gate? You can run and wait there for me to catch you up' or, 'Remember the bench halfway to the woods? You can run on ahead and wait for me there.' This activity should only be undertaken when you know it will be safe for the children to run on ahead and they can be trusted to stop in the right place. By learning a network of paths and key landmarks, children learn to expand their sense of position and space.

Idea 10.4   Repeated journeys

When children are young, the opportunity for repeated journeys allows them to develop their knowledge of the local landscape and the array of natural and man-made features. Having regular off-site excursions will give them walking experiences that develop this knowledge. Talking about where features are in relation to each other provides a relevant context for using the language of position and movement – for example, 'I know we are getting closer to the park when we pass the town hall.'

Many children enjoy drawing their journeys. As adults we can model how to annotate drawings and then use them for further discussions around position and movement. Regular journeys may include:

■ Visits to local shops to buy snacks.

■ Welly walks that explore the local neighbourhood.

■ Getting to and from a woodland or other greenspace site.

■ Walking between home and school. If the child comes by car, encourage parents and carers to park a little further away from the school to give children the opportunity to see and experience a local walk.

Encourage the children to recall their steps and the movement they made. This can be achieved by:

- Taking photos as prompts to help the children remember. These can be used to create a sequence or a book of the journey.

- Modelling where the children have been by placing sticks on the ground. It is also fun to model the journey using small world props. Bricks can represent houses, pine cones can indicate trees and so on.

- Using a sandpit where the journey is retraced in the sand.

Idea 10.5 Way finding

Involve children in plenty of conversations about knowing where the location of the group is and finding the destination. When walking out and about with a group, the adults can model stopping and asking for directions to the destination. This can be followed up by consulting a map (digital or paper), checking street signs and ensuring everyone is remembering the route being taken. Whilst satnav and other technology is useful, it is also helpful to encourage children to look at, remember and discuss locations.

There is an African proverb which says, 'Follow your nose.' Where will your group of children end up if they follow their noses? This can be another fun way to explore your local neighbourhood.

Idea 10.6 Visiting a play park

When at a park or play space, the children will use the equipment in lots of different ways. Take photos of individual children and talk about where they played using positional language as you look through the images.

- Look, you are *at the top* of the slide.

- Here you are sliding *down*.

- Now you are spinning *around* on the disc.

- Do you remember rocking *backwards* and *forwards*?

- I see you hiding *underneath* the slide. What was it like down there?

This activity also works well if a child has a favourite cuddly toy that can come along. The toy can be photographed in lots of different places in the playground. This can also be made into a simple book for the children.

Idea 10.7 Animal trails

Children enjoy observing the movements of animals. When they discover a slug, snail or other mini-beast, take the time to observe and comment on its movements and wonder where it is going. A follow-up to this can be challenging the children to move across a space like the animal.

Idea 10.8 Red Fox says …

Use a puppet or soft toy, such as a red fox, to give the children simple instructions such as, 'Red Fox says move two steps forward' and 'Now stretch your hands high up into the air.' If Red Fox does not give the instruction, then the children must not follow the action.

This can be extended to working with a partner. As the children become more proficient at playing the game, the instructions can become more complex, such as Red Fox says: 'Move in front of your partner.' 'Now move to the left of your partner.' 'Walk around your partner clockwise.'

Idea 10.9 Hunt the thimble

This traditional party game is easily adapted to any outdoor environment. All the children except one leave the space. The child left in the space has to 'hide' the thimble somewhere where it can be seen. The other children are invited back into the space and are guided towards the thimble by clues given by the child with the support of an adult – such as, 'Sam is getting nearer.' 'Oh, now he's moved further away.' 'Ahmed is now the closest.' The first child to find the thimble has the honour of hiding it the next time. The first child can stay in the space and help to advise. By doing this, each child in the group gets a turn at hiding the thimble.

Various adaptations of this game are easy to create: hiding a big teddy makes the game easier and using a natural object makes the game harder.

Idea 10.10 Washing line

If the children are washing clothes or other items and hanging them up to dry on a washing line, then seize the moment to play some guessing games. Give clues such as, 'This object is *in-between* the tea towel and the red trousers.' 'This object is *to the right* of teddy's jumper.' Objects or laminated pictures can also be pegged onto the washing line for similar activities.

Idea 10.11 Nature knots

This game is ideal for a calm autumn day. Collect lots of leaves in different colours (e.g. yellow, brown, green, red, orange). In a flat space, create a spinning board using a leaf of each colour and a pine cone as a spinner. Scatter the rest of the leaves close to each other nearby.

Each person in the game should stand on two leaves. When the pine cone is spun, each child should put a hand on the colour of leaf that the pine cone points to. Each time the spinner is spun, the children must move a hand or foot to a new leaf. If they fall over, they are out of the game.

The leaves can be moved closer or further apart to make the game easier or more challenging.

Idea 10.12 Obstacle courses

When the children create obstacle courses, challenge them to give instructions that use a range of positional language to each other or an adult. For example:

- Crawl through the tunnel.
- Climb up the ladder.
- Go over the top of the climbing frame.
- Jump down from the box.

If obstacle courses are a strong interest, then children may like adapting them to different themes.

■ Children enjoy pushing and pulling trolleys, suitcases and buggies through obstacle courses. They can fill these up with all sorts of objects – for example, the children may decide to transport stones dug up from the garden to a construction area at the other side of the outdoor space. Provide plenty of buckets if water is going to be transported and a big container for emptying the water into.

■ If you have hobby horses then show jumping courses are a lot of fun. If you don't have hobby horses the children will simply enjoy pretending to be ponies. Soft stretchy bandages can be deployed – one child is the horse and the bandages are the 'reins' which are held by the child behind.

■ Trikes or wheeled toys can be used for manoeuvring through obstacles. A Formula 1-style racing track can also be created.

■ Crufts and other dog shows provide inspiration for the children to set up dog challenges. Some children really enjoy pretending to be dogs! Others like a stick attached to a piece of string to become a 'dog'.

■ Herding sheep can be fun too. This is where one child is the shepherd, another is their dog and a small group of children hold hands and are the sheep who have to negotiate their way through the course. This works best if the children have had the opportunity to see a sheep dog in action.

■ Another activity for older children is to guide their partner, who pretends to be a robot, through an obstacle course one instruction at a time – for example, 'Take two steps forward. Turn towards the fence. Take one step forward.'

■ Challenge the children to move across the outdoor space without touching the ground.

■ Create mazes. This is particularly effective if the children have had experience of going through a maze in a local park.

Idea 10.13 Spiders' webs

Children love working their way through webs. In an area of your outdoor space, thread bandages or high visibility rope across in a three-dimensional way. The children will move under, over, around and through the strands. Have extra rope available so the children can make their own webs – so they can trap any super-villains, dinosaurs or other baddies who might be chasing them!

Idea 10.14 Trail making

Children are drawn towards making trails. Have resources ready for this activity and be prepared to model ideas if needed. Very often the purpose of a trail is to lead you to a place of interest such as a beautiful view, a cave or into a hole to meet a character (think of Michael Rosen's *We're Going On a Bear Hunt!*). Useful items include:

- Chalk
- High visibility rope, string or different colours of wool
- A range of small resources which won't blow away that link to children's interests (e.g. blocks, bricks, a bucket of shells, sticks, toy dinosaurs)
- Large planks or long branches which are light enough for the children to move

Create trails on wet sand using the heel of your foot or a stick. Add objects of interest to a sand trail. The children can draw these, make sandcastles, add piles of seaweed or create a simple shell pattern. The adult can use positional language as they walk through the trail the child has made and describe what can be seen along the way. In woodland areas, the abundance of sticks and other loose materials also allows for trails. Remember that trails can be micro or macro in size.

Idea 10.15 Shadow positions

If the children are fascinated with shadows, then investigations can happen which link the time of day to the length and position of shadows on a sunny day. Push an upright stick into the ground or into a bucket filled with soil or sand (alternatively, a fence post or similar will work). A child can carefully mark the shadow's length and position with a pegged piece of string.

Repeat this activity every hour using a new piece of string each time. The children will be able to see how the shadow moves and changes through the day. This is particularly interesting in winter when the shadows are longer. Does the length of the shadows change as well as the shape? In which directions do the shadows fall?

Idea 10.16 Compass bearings

Bearings are an abstract concept, so for very young children it is more appropriate to raise awareness rather than expect a comprehensive understanding. Adults can model the use of a compass when out and about as a means of way finding. Having the four compass points indicated somewhere in the outdoor space can be helpful. The directions can then be referred to when relevant to routines, children's interests and ongoing work. For example:

- Describing the location of different objects in the outdoor space and features in the environment beyond it.

- Discussing where seeds and plants should be positioned.

- Noticing areas of sunlight and shadow. North-facing outdoor spaces will have more shadows than south-facing ones.

- Deciding where to do certain activities that need sunlight or shade.

- Linking to shadow play and observing the direction in which shadows are falling (see Idea 10.15).

Idea 10.17 Spin the pine cone

Using a compass to locate the bearings, mark the points north, south, east and west on the ground. In the centre place a large pine cone and check that it can spin easily. The children take turns to spin the cone. When it points to a bearing, the children must run and touch a feature in the landscape in that direction.

CHAPTER 11

Data Handling

Data handling enables the development of ideas, discussions and investigations across all subject areas within and beyond maths. Children's questions and observations can be explored through data handling – the mathematical approach provides a framework for practical problem-solving and talking about the experiences. Data handling is also the beginnings of statistics.

Much can happen spontaneously as a result of what children find or wonder about when outside. Data handling makes the most of children's innate curiosity and need to explore and discover the world around them. Working outdoors enables children to experience a broader range of information handling opportunities including:

- Developing practical field study skills.

- Collecting real world data about the immediate environment.

- Presenting information in different ways (e.g. through the use of natural materials *in situ*).

- Creating bigger representations of data outside, beyond the use of digital or pencil and paper activities.

- Adapting and using any form of picture or diagram for organising or displaying data outside.

The skills of matching, sorting and collecting go hand in hand with children's development. Our brains process and make sense of information through associations; categorising and classifying what we see, hear, feel, taste and smell. Our homes are organised so that we can store, find and retrieve items we need. If we observe children playing and see how they collect, sort, match and classify toys and other objects, then we can develop meaningful ways of extending their learning mathematically based upon their schematic knowledge of the world.

According to Zoe Rhydderch-Evans there are four critical questions that children should learn to answer when it comes to developing their data-handling knowledge and skills:[1]

- What do I want or need to know?

- How am I going to get the information I need?

- How am I going to organise and represent the information?

- What did I find out?

Data handling does not have to involve extensive learning investigations. There is a place for simple activities, such as sorting finds after going for a walk or recording the scores in a game, in

---

1 Z. Rhydderch-Evans, *Mathematics in the School Grounds* (Exmouth: Southgate Publishers, 1993), p. 40.

which only one aspect of data handling need be used as a tool for enabling discussions or further investigations.

Adults need to ensure that:

■ A range of data-handling opportunities happen based upon children asking a pertinent question or discovering a matter that needs further investigation.

■ Numerical as well as graphical representations of data are facilitated. Both kinds of thinking and representing are significant and help with the interpretation of information gathered.

■ Links are made between concrete experiences, the use of symbols to create data and pictorial representations of these experiences. Time should also be made to discuss and consider what has been learnt or discovered.

■ The children practise how to sketch specific tables, charts, diagrams and other methods of recording information.

■ The children are able to develop their own ways and means of recording, so that their confidence in their own abilities grows. They should be actively involved at every step in the decision-making about the gathering, organising and presenting of information.

Vocabulary

Alike, belongs, bigger than, chart, classify, collect, column, diagram, difference between, display, does not belong, few, fewer, fewest, first, gather, graph, greatest, group, how many, least, less than, match, more than, odd one out, order, organise, row, similar, smaller than, sort, tally, the same as, tick, total, vote

Expressions

Sort something out

Mix and match items

Put your life in order

Display good behaviour

Idea **11.1** It's all about people

Children can be the data. They can stand in sets, move up and down lines and represent their thoughts in real time with the choice of where they stand. The advantage of this technique is that people can be used in any environment and the physical movement can help the children to understand more about data handling. The disadvantage is that sometimes the scale is too big and the children can't see the whole picture when they are part of it.

Idea 11.2 Grouping children for a walk or other activities

When the children are organised into small groups for a walk, each group will be distinct if the children stay with that group and a key adult. The 'data' is a concrete experience. Each child will stand with their designated adult. During the course of a year, show the children different ways of representing this information pictorially – for example, group photos or a table with lists of children under the name of each adult.

To move from three-dimensional to two-dimensional representations, each group should begin by standing in their own circle formed from a rope or chalk outline. Each child draws a cross or puts down a stone in the circle. When the children leave the circle, a pictorial image of each group is left on the ground, indicated by the crosses or stones within the circle. You could spend time as a whole class looking at the group circles on the ground:

- Count the number of people in each group.

- Does every group have the same number of children?

- Do some groups have more or fewer children?

Idea 11.3 Venn diagram reflections

Moving on from the groupings in Idea 11.2, the children can discuss their thoughts about their groups after the walk. Did the groupings work well? What needs to be changed next time?

Use ropes or chalk to create two intersecting sets to represent a Venn diagram. The children stand in the part of the diagram that represents their opinion or interests. For example, following a visit to a woodland you might place a photo or object to represent tree climbing in one set and den building in the other. The children have to think about what they did and where to stand. If a child did both activities then they stand in the intersecting set. If some children did neither activity then they stand outside both sets. It is important that they are represented too.

Idea 11.4 Creating human graphs when lining up

Human graphs can be used when the children line up. An adult or a child can make a simple closed request such as, 'If you are wearing green, line up here. If you are not wearing green, then line up there.' A variety of mathematical discussions can ensue:

- Which line has the largest/smallest number of children? How can we work this out?

- What does this tell us?

- How many more children are wearing green? How can we work this out?

- What other ideas do you have for lining up?

You can develop this activity through:

- Encouraging the children to choose and ask questions. They can also learn how to lead aspects of lining up, such as counting the number of children in each line or asking everyone to hold hands so that it is easier to work out how many more children are in one line than the other.

- Lining up on numbers, tiles or slabs where each child can stand on one tile.

Idea 11.5 Become a curator

If a child wants to bring in a collection of objects to show the group then, where relevant, ask them to create a display outside – some collections are naturally outdoorsy. Ask them for their reasons for setting out items in a particular way – that is to say, sorting and classifying their collections. How will they house their collections?

- How would a child create a fairy world for fairies to live in? Which fairies will live where?

- A 'Jurassic Park' island is needed for any visiting dinosaurs. How will the children keep the carnivorous dinosaurs from eating the herbivores?

- What sort of miniature world would Lego characters require?

- Can the children build a multistorey car park or garage for visiting toy cars?

Find out from parents and carers if they have any relevant collections and whether they would be willing to bring some examples to your nursery and talk about them with the children. For example:

- Bird watchers keep notes about and photos of the birds they see.

- Rock hounds collect rocks.

- Rock climbers have interesting kit, including karabiners, slings and 'friends'.

Idea 11.6 What makes a shop a shop?

Going for a walk along a high street can be interesting. Children will enjoy sharing their experiences of visiting different shops and explaining why they liked them. Beforehand, consider together what makes a shop a shop and create a list of ideas. This could be used to create a visual tick list. Afterwards, review the list and amend it according to what the children have learnt. Work out what all shops have in common.

Similar questions can be applied to any interest a child may have, for example:

- What makes a tree a tree?

- What makes a worm a worm?

- What makes a house a house?

By identifying similarities, rules are being created that enable children to sort and classify the world around them according to agreed criteria.

Idea 11.7 Be a sifter and a sorter

Many years ago I worked for an archaeology company. My job was to search through sieved soil to extract tiny finds such as grains, pottery shards and other interesting items. I had to categorise them, label the finds and send any important ones to specialists for further examination. This idea can be adapted easily to work in a tuff tray or shoebox filled with dry soil. Provide magnifiers to help the children see what is hidden in the soil and bowls or plates for placing their found treasures in. This is particularly valuable if you know an archaeologist who can visit or if you are able to arrange a visit to a local dig.

Tiny items are a source of fascination for children. Encourage miniature collections to be developed that fit in matchboxes and require sorting with tweezers.

Idea 11.8 Collecting data about the natural world

Develop simple charts so the children can record their findings and observations. Once they know what to do, the charts can be left in bird hide dens, beside log piles or mini-beast hotels, or placed near a pond for ongoing survey work. Examples include:

■ Photo collections of local wildlife. I have created little laminated booklets for the children to look at, take apart and sort as they wish. These include sets of birds, flowers, mini-beasts and animals. Similar sets could be created for man-made collections such as car logos or aeroplanes.

■ Simple tick charts. Rather than start with a table, give each bird a strip. The children put a tick in order in the boxes when they sight that bird. This means that the results can be transformed into either a chart or a graph as the ticks are evenly spaced.

	1	2	3	4	5
Blue Tit					
Robin					

- Spotters' guides. The Woodland Trust Nature Detectives website has lots of downloadable charts and spotters' guides for this purpose.[2] The sheets have several photos, each with a tick box beside it.

- Citizen science surveys. The Open Air Laboratories (OPAL) network has several citizen science projects which involve children collecting information and uploading it to their website.[3] The bug count survey is geared towards younger children. Free packs are provided including identification charts and viewing lenses.

---

2 See: http://www.woodlandtrust.org.uk/naturedetectives/.

3 See: http://www.opalexplorenature.org.

Collecting and sorting objects

Many simple data-handling activities can be undertaken through collecting objects and bringing them back to a gathering circle for games that involve sorting, classifying and comparing. This helps children to develop the vocabulary needed to describe attributes such as shape, species, size, weight, colour and texture. It can also be used to model various mathematical representations such as diagrams, sets, pictograms and different graphs.

Idea 11.9 Find something interesting

I often kick-start a group get-together by asking the children to 'find something interesting'. This is always preceded by a short discussion about what is okay and what is not okay to bring back to the gathering circle.

Ask the group to think about how the finds could be sorted (e.g. by colour). The displays may not follow expected mathematical layouts, such as a Venn diagram. However, the discussions which arise can be insightful and provide further understanding into how children sort, classify and match objects.

Idea 11.10 | Interest sheet sorting

Children often pick things up when out and about. It is worth providing a small bag for this purpose so that valued finds can be transported easily. Set up an interest sheet (an old white cloth) so the children can place their treasures on the sheet to be discussed or shared at an appropriate time. You could use the opportunity to model different ways of sorting.

- Have one hoop or rope circle on the sheet for one type of object chosen by a child (e.g. leaves). The rest of the sheet may contain any other objects of interest (i.e. not leaves).

- Make two hoops or rope circles intersect with one another. Let the children decide what attributes go in each circle. For instance, a child may choose 'yellow' and 'leaves'. Any objects without these properties must stay outside the hoops but remain on the sheet.

- Put three baskets with labels agreed by the children (e.g. sticks, cones and leaves) on the sheet. Any other items are placed on the sheet.

Idea 11.11 | My object belongs here

This open-ended game helps children to develop the confidence to explain their decisions about classifying and sorting. It may take several goes before they get the hang of the game, so persevere. Each child finds and brings an object to the interest sheet. In a random order, the children place their object on the sheet and explain their decision for the precise placement of it. One object needs to be put down first to help everyone get going. For example:

- I'm putting my leaf beside this leaf as they are both leaves.

- I'm putting my stone far away from the leaves because it is different.

- I'm putting my leaf near to the other leaves, but not right beside because it is a different colour.

If a child isn't able to give a reason when they put an object on the sheet, ask other children in the group for their ideas on why the object can stay where it has been placed.

Idea 11.12 Logic squares

This is a version of twenty questions. Ask each child in the group to find an object which is no bigger than their hands to put into a grid akin to a noughts and crosses layout. Start with no more than nine objects.

The children take it in turns to ask a question which can only be answered with 'yes' or 'no'. It can help if these are prepared on cards beforehand. For example:

Is the object natural?	Yes – remove all the man-made objects No – remove all the natural objects
Is the object a stone?	Yes – remove all the other objects No – remove all the stones
Is the object grey?	Yes – remove all the other coloured stones No – remove all the grey stones

This activity naturally leads on to exploring sorting through the use of Carroll diagrams (see Idea 11.21).

Idea 11.13 Odd one out

With collections of objects, invent odd one out games. This helps the children to spot the difference and observe transformations. This may involve:

■ A puppet or fantasy character coming along and adding a rogue item to a collection.

■ Creating a line of objects that contains an item which doesn't belong in the collection.

■ Adding an item to the collection.

■ Playing the game on a grid and seeing if this helps the children to notice and make changes.

As the children's visual perception skills improve, then make the changes more subtle. Depending on your collection, you could:

■ Rotate one object through half a turn.

- Turn one object over.

- Move one object to a different place on the sheet.

- Switch the order of objects in a line.

- Replace an object with one which is the same, except that it is a different size, colour or type.

Matching games

Matching objects helps children to recognise similarities and differences between them. This might be direct matching of three-dimensional objects or the marrying of attributes such as size, shape, type or colour. In mathematical terms, we are helping the children to learn about equivalence (what is the same about a group of objects) and transformation (what is different about a group of objects).

Practitioners, children and parents can brainstorm together to create a bank of matching games. Be aware of the level of complexity of each game and encourage the children to think about how they could change the rules and contribute towards making a game more challenging and enjoyable. You will be surprised at their ideas. Also, once a game has been introduced to a group, they can learn to play it with a partner or in a smaller group to promote independence. What follows are some ideas to get you going.

Idea 11.14 Flowerpot pairs

You will need twenty-four flowerpots or similar containers that can be turned upside down to cover an object. Collect up to twelve pairs of objects. Hide each object under a flowerpot laid out in an array. The children take turns to lift up two flowerpots to see if they have found a pair. When this happens, the flowerpot and the object is removed and kept by the child. Once all the pairs have been found, the children count how many pairs of objects they have won. To make the game easier, use fewer objects. Alternatively, create two arrays of twelve items with one object from each pair in each array.

Idea 11.15 Leaf snap

Each child who wants to play gathers approximately five different leaves and brings them to the gathering circle where they sit with their pile of leaves in front of them. In turn, each child places a leaf onto a white sheet. As soon as a match is made with someone else, the first person to call 'snap' can collect both leaves.

Idea 11.16 Elmer's colours

Outside, the variety of different tones of colour is significant, so colour matching becomes more challenging. After reading a story, such as David McKee's 'Elmer the Patchwork Elephant', the children may wish to:

- Pick their favourite colour to find outside.

- Look at the colours they are wearing and try to find a similar natural colour outside.

- Pick one colour and search for lots of different shades.

On a white sheet at the gathering circle, set up hoops or baskets to enable the children to sort their finds by colour.

Idea 11.17 Same and different

For this game, put the objects on a white sheet and gather everyone around. The children take turns to pick up two of the objects and ask the rest of the group, 'What's the same about these things?' The others have to come up with suggestions. Next, the child asks, 'What's different?' and the others have to come up with suggestions.

Idea 11.18 More of the same

Each child has to 'find something interesting which is no bigger than your hand' and bring the object to the gathering circle. The object is then swapped with another child. The challenge is to find someone with the same object so that there is now a pair of each object. Afterwards, the number of objects collected can be counted in twos.

Idea 11.19 Nature dominoes

The children can create their own set of dominoes from natural materials. This works best on a dry day. Provide rectangular pieces of cardboard with a middle line drawn in permanent marker pen. Stick double-sided sticky tape on either side. The children can add their choice of found objects, placing one on each side of the middle line. Once several dominoes have been made, the children can try to create a domino line in which the objects are matched in sequence.

Idea 11.20 Tick or tally charts

Tick charts tend to precede tally charts for measuring the frequency of an event or the numbers of an item being recorded. One tick represents each item recorded. They are sometimes called frequency tables.

Ticks or tally marks can be taught to children when playing games so they learn how to keep score. For example, a popular game is to draw a circle on the ground and then draw a line a few steps away for the children to stand behind. The children each have to throw a stick so that it lands in the circle. Show the children how to put a mark by a child's name or photo on a clipboard if they are successful. Count up the number of marks and celebrate the whole group's efforts.

When creating tally charts outside, sticks can be used to represent each mark. This can help the children to make the leap from using three-dimensional objects to two-dimensional representations. For example, a group may be walking in the forest. At a turning, the children have to decide which part of the woodland they wish to visit. As a way of voting, each child can find a stick and lay it in the row which reflects their choice:

Place	Tally	Total
The deep dark wood	IIIII II	7
The wood by the stream	IIIII	5

The tally marks can be grouped in fives so the children learn how to group to enable quick counting to happen, and to help them learn how to count on rather than simply starting counting from one each time.

Idea 11.21 Carroll diagrams

Carroll diagrams involve sorting objects according to defined attributes based upon what objects are and are not. It begins with discrete sets where there is no overlap. To introduce the concept of a Carroll diagram, it is useful to begin with two sets: what something is and what it is not. The objects can be laid out with clear labels:

Green	Not green

This can be extended to a 2 x 2 Carroll diagram by the addition of an extra row, as indicated in the photo below.

Once the children are used to sorting and displaying information in this way, progress to attributes such as colour (red, not red), size (small, not small), shape (long, not long), texture (smooth, not smooth) or number (three, not three).

Encourage the children to think of their own ideas for Carroll diagrams and provide sorting hoops, buckets and opportunities to enable this to happen. For example, a child may notice that some shells in a bag are broken. They can sort the shells into those that are broken and those that aren't. Another extension is to invite the children to turn their sorted objects into collages or pictures.

Idea **11.22** Simple pictograms

Pictograms use objects, photos or graphics to help children identify and record information. A blank cloth grid is helpful as children may struggle to line up collected objects correctly when they are different sizes.

Idea 11.23 Probability, chance and certainty

The likelihood of an event happening is the sort of conversation young children want and need to engage with – it helps them to understand and cope with change. It is useful for taking calculated risks through knowing people and places. It is about making sensible decisions and choices. It is also helpful when it comes to making judgements and deciding on a course of action.

Mathematically, probability is a form of estimation and reasoning. It develops from initially subjective and non-quantitative ideas to thinking and reasoning in a numerical and statistical way. Professions such as financial forecasting and pursuits such as gambling rely on sophisticated mathematical thinking. In many other occupations, such as structural engineering, climbing or even gardening, we use our knowledge of chance to make informed decisions.

Children enjoy discussions and opportunities to engage positively with a range of predicted outcomes. They will hear about and perhaps even directly experience unusual happenings, both good and bad. Likewise, there are routines and sequences of events that are certainties in our lives. Probability is a continuum which ranges from certain to uncertain with variations between these two extremes.

Whilst this aspect of maths is often ignored in the early years, we can lay the foundations for later formal experiences in several ways:

■ Play games which rely on chance to win or which involve an element of luck. These can be used to help children discuss the chances of winning, the likelihood of throwing a six and so on.

■ Make time for conversations with children about likelihood. Encourage them to justify their suggestions. This helps them to realise that probability, chance and uncertainty are concepts that can be discussed and analysed. Link these to real events and activities. For example, when talking about the weather you can bring up questions such as:

   O Is there anything about today's weather which we can say is very likely or unlikely? How do we know?

   O It has been sunny every day this week, what do you think the weather will be like tomorrow? Is it likely that it will snow?

   O What makes you so sure about this?

   O How do we know this for certain?

Note the vocabulary used and model this yourself: fair, unfair, certain, uncertain, never, definitely, maybe, chance and so on.

CHAPTER 12

Routines

Many educators worry about making sufficient time for maths on a daily basis. One of the most effective ways of doing so is through examining the routines that exist in your establishment and infusing these with maths. Once a routine is established, it can be easy to spot the child who needs assistance or who is ready for more complex maths and to make these adjustments. You can back-link the learning within the routine to your curriculum. Your children will be the evidence of this learning. For example, a child who can sing the hand-washing song as a cue for how long to wash their hands is demonstrating a non-standardised approach to measuring time.

Idea 12.1 : Visual voting systems

Put a voting system in place which allows the children to decide which outdoor activity they enjoyed doing that day. Place flowerpots beside each outdoor activity or area and ask the children to put a laminated photo of themselves in the pot beside their favourite activity towards the end of a session. This is great for starting discussions about what the children like to do outside. The results can be counted and displayed on the ground as sets, a pictograph or other representation. The discussions and choices can then be used to plan the next steps for individuals or groups of children.

Idea 12.2 : Visual timetables and registration

- When self-registering, the children can add their name to a number line so it is easy to work out the number of children present. A simple approach is to take a blank number track and the children can add a stone with their picture or name on it. It helps them to see and use a number line.

- How many stones have a combined mass of one kilogramme? Put a kilogramme weight into a bucket balance. The children can register by adding their name stone to the bucket. Parents and children can enjoy seeing which child's stone hits the magic weight. This can lead to discussions and investigations about the mass of all the children's stones and how heavy they are.

Provide an outdoor visual timetable used with and by the children. Have photographs or symbols representing different activities that are available in the different areas outside. Remember to keep making the link to the time displayed on an analogue clock. In due course children get adept at knowing the key times of the day and where the hands will be on the clock.

- Use a stick covered with Velcro to attach and order different cards. Alternatively, hang cards or wood cookies from a horizontal stick.

- Use a washing line and peg up the activities. Ask the children to help you create the timetable on a daily basis.

- Set alarms to indicate key times or events. These need not be intrusive sounds given the wide choice available on smartphones and tablets.

Take time at the start or end of a session to look at the visual timetable with the children so they know what events are happening each day. It can be a useful tool to review what happened the previous day and talk about what is going to happen tomorrow. It is also an opportunity to discuss the date and days of the week and to compare time intervals.

Idea 12.3 Developing a sense of time through routines

There are lots of uses of time within the context of routines:

- Using a sand-timer to facilitate taking turns and encouraging the children to do this without the need for adult intervention.

- Singing a song to get ready to go out, wash hands or during tidy-up time can help the children to develop their sense of time.

- Counting aloud and comparing this to a timer – for example, counting a steady pace such as 'one caterpillar', 'two caterpillars' up to ten and then comparing this to the number of seconds that have passed.

Idea 12.4 Timelines and sequencing books

Create timelines and books featuring sequences of activities that the children do outside. Include different periods of time such as short activities, a full session in nursery and weekly or monthly events. For example:

- How we wash our hands outside

- Making a mud cake

- Our morning at nursery

- On Monday we …, on Tuesday we … and so on

- Autumn in our local woods

Digital books can be made using a variety of story-making apps. However, ensure that some books are printed out and laminated for use outside. In particular, create sequencing cards which can be pegged up on a washing line. This enables the children to look at the photos, sort and order them and engage in conversations about time whilst doing so.

Idea 12.5 The weather

There are commercial manual weather recorders available from education suppliers. These can be a good source of discussion with children as to whether it feels hot or cold outside and how this relates to the seasons. Sometimes children like making their own weather stations with rain gauges made from plastic bottles, simple wind vanes, thermometers and weather stones. Search online for ideas. Homemade weather equipment makes the data collection more meaningful.

At the early level, children will need practice at putting objects into different graphs, charts and displays to represent the weather. Simple weather charts can be displayed in picture form.

This week's weather	Monday	Tuesday	Wednesday	Thursday	Friday
Sun					
Rain					
Wind					
Clouds					
Other					

Idea 12.6 Changing routines

When getting ready to go outside, the children often have to put on outdoor clothing. This provides an opportunity to focus on some routines involving maths:

- One-to-one correspondence: one hat goes on one head.
- One-to-two correspondence: one pair of trousers needs two legs.
- Two-to-two correspondence: two arms go into two sleeves.
- The buttons are counted to check they have all been done up.
- Compare, with due sensitivity to the children's feelings, the different sizes of outdoor clothing: wellies, gloves and so on. Show the children how to do this accurately when putting on or taking off these items. Encourage them to find the missing one of a pair.
- Hang outdoor clothing on hangers. In this way, the children learn to ensure items are balanced when hung up on a rail so that they do not fall off. This is a practical application of equivalence in mass.

- The children can pack their backpacks and estimate whether they have enough room for all their items when going on a walk, thereby developing their concept of three-dimensional space.

- Sequencing photos of getting dressed and undressed can be put on display to help the children remember the easiest order and thus what needs to be done first, second and so on.

Idea 12.7 The messy cloakroom

A messy cloakroom is a practical data-handling challenge. Help the children to consider what is involved in the tidying up process.

- Request that the children first take photos for the all-important 'before' and 'after' effect.

- How will they sort the clothing and footwear? Will it be by size, colour or another way?

- How will the space be reorganised? Are baskets needed for gloves? What will serve as a hat stand? If there aren't enough pegs, what can the children use or do instead to arrange the clothing?

- Once the cloakroom is shipshape, take 'after' photos. What do the children think of their efforts?

Over the following weeks, keep evaluating the effectiveness of the new system. If something isn't working well, have another brainstorm and keep at it until you have a system which works.

Idea 12.8 Setting up the outdoor space

If you and your children have to set up an outdoor space from scratch each day, then use this as an opportunity to develop different maths concepts.

Developing an awareness of shape, position and movement

- Which objects need to be pushed or pulled into the correct position?

- What needs to be rotated or turned around to make it balance properly or be fixed safely?

- Do any set-ups have a mirror line or create a natural axis of symmetry?

- What can be used to develop a sense of perspective? For example, setting up a tall climbing frame for height.

Developing an understanding of measurement

■ Which items feel the heaviest to move and which are the lightest and easiest? Some objects may simply be too heavy to move.

■ The children can help to set up water canisters for outdoor use. Fill them with varying amounts of water and let the children experience the weight of different volumes of water.

■ Hammocks, nets and rope swings need to be erected so they are the right height above the ground. How do we ensure this is accurate?

■ Put up simple pulley systems (see Idea 6.17).

Integrating pattern into the space

■ The bags used for taking resources outside could be stored and laid out in a specific pattern according to different attributes, such as size, shape, colour or number of objects stored in the bag.

■ Tyres can be rolled into a line relating to size (e.g. little, big, little, big, or in pairs if your tyres have been acquired in pairs).

■ Kitchen utensils and other equipment in sand, water or mud areas can be laid out in a clear pattern, such as by size, material, colour, purpose or other attributes decided by the children.

■ Items can be hung to dry on a washing line using a pattern of coloured pegs. Peg different coloured socks or other objects on a washing line for the children to order and reorder (see Idea 10.10).

■ Have sufficient big and small containers to allow for size-based patterns in the sand, water or mud area (e.g. five mud pies all in a row!).

■ Present displays so a pattern can be seen explicitly, such as a circular pattern of objects.

Idea 12.9 Tidying up

Tidying up throws up lots of mathematical problems, so ensure the children have plenty of opportunities to get involved.

■ Pack away toys into fixed containers – for example, a milk crate might house all the mud area kitchen utensils. Other objects may need to be put inside boxes. What items fit best into the different containers?

■ Draw children's attention to objects which need to be stacked when tidying up. This could be plates, plastic cups, wooden blocks, chairs, bread crates, milk crates and pallets.

- Fold material, such as tarps, den building and dressing-up materials, and put them away in a smaller space such as an old suitcase. Draw attention to the instructions and model the language such as 'fold', 'half' and so on. Ask the children what they observe happening as the tarp is being folded up and listen to their language and understanding. Discuss the shapes being created at each fold and their changing size. Look at different ways of folding the same tarp. It is a good moment to talk about the similarities of the shapes as they change and what differences the children notice.

- Roll up items to store them. Rope, string, scarves, bandages and other similar items can be rolled or coiled, so the children can begin to learn that length is conserved when this happens.

- Review ways of sorting and grouping – for example, types of toys, toys that stack and toys that roll.

Idea 12.10 Lining up

When the children line up, discuss order, position and place with them:

- Who is in front of whom?
- Who is beside whom?
- Who is behind you?

- Who is diagonally opposite you?
- Who are you paired with?

There are links to ordinal numbers here – who is first, second, third and so on. You can also reference number order including the numbers before, after and in-between.

Idea 12.11 Marian's magic number

Marian Cairns, a former early years adviser, developed this simple approach to head counts. When going on a walk or off-site visit, the group can identify its 'magic number'. This is the total number of children and adults in the group. Involve the children in counting the number of people before setting off. When the group is called to come together, the children can use the magic number to check that everyone is present. This can happen in different ways to develop the children's counting skills:

■ A soft toy or stick is passed around the circle. The children count aloud together as this happens.

■ An adult or child walks around the outside of the circle and gently taps each person on the shoulder as everyone counts aloud.

■ The children speak their number in turn.

Idea 12.12 Making a circle

When calling children to the gathering circle or to gain their attention, use identifiable sound patterns or a song. You can time the group to see how quickly they can come.

Make a circle using a rope. The children can hold on to it and learn to gently pull it tight. Next, lay it on the ground. You can then talk about who is beside whom. For this purpose, I often use a puppet who wants to know:

■ The name of someone standing to the left.

■ Who is standing in-between child X and child Y.

■ Who is sitting opposite child A.

Emphasise the direction of travel when taking turns, passing objects or running around the outside of the circle – clockwise or anticlockwise.

Put electrical tape at one metre intervals on the rope so the children begin to develop the concept of one metre. It is useful for quickly creating large circles and ensuring that the children are evenly spaced out.

Stones on logs

During an adventure, each child picks up a stone. When leaving the gathering circle, they each place their stone on a log to show how many children have left. When they come back they remove their stone to show they are back. This is helpful for learning to count forwards and backwards.

Niki Buchan, education consultant, Natural Learning

Idea 12.13 Warming up outside

If children are feeling cold or have been sitting for a while, play some warm-up games.

Funky chicken

- Wave one hand in the air, jump up and down, and count on each jump: 'One, two, three, four.'

- Swap hands and repeat the action, counting up to four.

- Next, stick one foot out and hop whilst counting up to four.

- Change feet and count up to four.

Repeat all of the above but only count up to three. Then repeat and only count to two. Finally, count just the number one. Finish by jumping in the air and shouting 'Funky chicken!' and wave both hands.

Action numbers

Develop actions linked to numbers called out in sequence:

1   Touch the ground

2   Stretch up high

3   Star jump

Children enjoy choosing the actions for this activity. They can also be adapted to illustrate the movements of animals or birds.

Idea **12.14** Outdoor snack

- As part of a picnic, barbecue or campfire, add numbers to items such as cups which can be put out in order or counted to check the correct number are there. Establish whether the number of snack items matches the number of children and adults present.

- Have signs in self-help snack areas that indicate the number of pieces of fruit the children can help themselves to at a time (e.g. two pieces of apple, ten raisins, three pieces of banana). They can always come back for seconds if they have finished and would like more.

- Look for opportunities to double the quantities. For example, if children are toasting marshmallows, it may be decided that they need two each. Also think about the sets of cups, crockery and cutlery required.

- When preparing snacks, focus on patterns: the sequence of vegetables on a kebab stick, the pouring of a sauce in a pattern over a pancake, the decoration on a cake or biscuits.

- Go to a local shop, market or supermarket with a group of children to buy some fruit and vegetables for snacks. Each child could pick a loose item, such as mushrooms, potatoes or tomatoes, and weigh it before buying. Have a conversation based around the weight and mass of the vegetables and fruit being weighed.

Idea **12.15** The language of position

When snacks are being laid out, ask the children to put certain items in certain places. For example, when setting up a fire pit for cooking snacks, you can provide instructions such as:

- Put the snacks in a line.
- We need the skewers next to the red peppers.
- The water bucket goes beside the fire.
- Place the bin at the end of the row.

Idea 12.16 | The sharing opportunities of an outdoor snack

Much conversation can be had around what to cut up or share out and how this can be done equally. The children could:

- Lay out a picnic and share out the plates, cups and cutlery.

- Cut up and serve slices of pizza made in an outdoor oven.

- Split and share fruit such as bananas.

- Make soup over a campfire and share it. If there is any left over this can be given to another group of children.

- Open up peas in pods and share out the peas between the group. Share other vegetables as they are dug up or harvested.

Idea 12.17 Snack subtraction story games

Eating snacks outside is an ideal time to make up subtraction stories and play games associated with eating. For example, you could begin by counting the number of pieces of fruit on your own plate. Then tell the story of a hungry caterpillar who eats one piece of fruit. You can wriggle your finger and pretend it is a caterpillar. Ask the children how many pieces of fruit you now have left on your plate. The children can then decide how many pieces of fruit their caterpillar will eat and how many will be left over. Repeat the process until all the fruit on the plate has been eaten.

Idea 12.18 Pay for snacks

Make the children 'pay' for snacks with coins. The children should collect the required amount from one part of the nursery (the coins can be stuck to a display board) and take it to the snack area where another child must check that it is the correct amount. This works especially well if snacks are available outside from a market, street stall or other outdoor enterprise.

As the children's confidence in handling money develops, they may have to pay for each item separately. For example, a hot dog may cost two pence and milk may cost five pence. What coins will the children need if something costs six pence?

Idea 12.19 Buy snacks from a shop

Take a group of children to a local shop to buy the food needed to make a snack. Pay in cash and get the children to help you count out the money. This can be particularly effective if they have researched online how much a chosen item costs and then have to consider which coins they need. At the shop, each child can find their item and pay for it.

If you have to use a bank card, talk with the children about the need to look after a card and keep it safe. Show the children how to cover your hand as you type in the number to pay for items or withdraw money from a bank. Let them know that the number is not shared with anyone else.

CHAPTER 13

The Mathematical Garden

Friedrich Froebel (1782–1852) is widely acknowledged as having developed the concept of a kindergarten as 'a garden of, and for, growing children'.[1] He advocated play, valued gardening and other outdoor pursuits and believed that children should have the freedom to grow and develop intellectually as well as physically.

Froebel developed what are believed to be the first educational toys, which he called 'Gifts'. These were only presented to a child when they were developmentally ready to receive them. The Gifts are highly symbolic and represent the unity of the laws of nature. They are mathematical forms, beginning with three-dimensional solids and moving on to two-dimensional shapes. As children grow, the Gifts progress and become increasingly complex. Through playing and exploring the Gifts, children develop their understanding of abstract concepts: 'From objects to pictures, from pictures to symbols, from symbols to ideas, leads the ladder of knowledge'.[2]

This is similar to the views of the maths education experts outlined in the Introduction. Froebel clearly understood the need for children to learn simultaneously through mathematical explorations and outdoor experiences in open-ended ways.

In line with Froebel's unified way of thinking, it is perhaps time to consider more precisely the role of maths in connecting the outdoor world with children's inner selves. The totality of a child's development thrives on satisfying their intellectual, emotional and physical needs.

For many years I have mused over the concept of a 'mathematical garden', a place that has been deliberately created to stimulate

1 See: R. Joyce, *Outdoor Learning: Past and Present* (Maidenhead: Open University Press, 2012), p. 52.

2 See: http://froebelgifts.com.

mathematical thinking and outside play. It is rare to find an education establishment that has given specific thought as to how the design of an outdoor space can enhance the mathematics that takes place there, beyond traditional playground markings.

Yet, with the growth of outdoor nurseries, the question must also be asked about whether artificial spaces are needed. Perhaps a mathematical garden is, in fact, a wilder space or a metaphor for seeing the mathematical value in any space or place. Very often a few tweaks are all that is needed rather than an expensive transformation. Any changes need to have value, purpose and meaning for children. The UK school grounds charity, Learning through Landscapes, advocates involving them in every step of the way in a participatory process.[3] This chapter explores the physical changes that you can make to an outdoor space.

The orientation of your outdoor space

Orientation is about the amount and type of vertical and horizontal spaces. It is helpful to think about the orientation of every feature as well as the space as a whole. Children need to be able to see their space from a range of perspectives and consider the affordance of different materials and features.

---

3 See: http://www.ltl.org.uk.

Idea 13.1 Horizontal spaces – levels

Levels are important in order for children to experience space. These include horizontal working surfaces at different heights. With some features, such as water, sand, mud and garden areas, adding levels increases the affordance of the space – that is, the open-ended possibilities. Try putting a table into or beside a sandpit and see the impact on how children use the space. Think about how you can provide the following range of levels.

Below ground level

This is useful for considering the concept of negative numbers – options include:

■ A place to dig down into the ground

■ Sunken pits that house cones, gravel, sand or other loose materials

■ Puddles

Height

Adding height into an outdoor space provides a viewpoint so children can look down on their surroundings, experience scale and perspective, and develop their spatial awareness – options include:

■ A hill

■ A tree which can be climbed

■ Fixed playground equipment

■ A small ladder to move around and use for climbing

Children also need to stretch and reach which often involves estimation and consideration of the likelihood of being able to do so. This can happen through:

■ Tree climbing

■ Placing some resources a little higher than eye level which involves a stretch to reach (e.g. a canister of water with a tap hung up for children to collect water)

■ Hanging resources, mobiles and constructions (see Idea 6.15)

Idea 13.2 | Inclines

Inclines help children to explore speed, distance and time. Children may travel around an outdoor space on wheeled vehicles or transport objects using trolleys or suitcases. A range of toys, shapes and objects can be stored near a slope to facilitate play involving rolling items. Use milk crates and other stackable objects in combination with guttering and planks to create small-scale slopes.

Idea 13.3 | Vertical spaces

Children need vertical spaces such as latticing, walls, fences and hedges to look through, to provide privacy, to stretch up and peek over, to attach things to and to poke items through. Temporary vertical spaces can be created through hanging up materials and partitioning using raised beds (see Idea 2.7 for additional resource suggestions).

Idea 13.4 | Holes

Children like to put things in holes, which are three-dimensional hollow spaces (see also Idea 9.6). Creating holes of various shapes and sizes and on various levels adds to children's play experiences of volume, capacity and space. Possibilities include:

- Posting boxes of different sorts.

- Holes in fences to peek through, talk to friends through, thread hoses through or post objects through. A friendly joiner may be able to create simple wooden shapes which can be matched and posted through holes in panels. This helps children to learn informally about rotational symmetry.

- Tunnels which are long holes that can be crawled through.

It can be interesting to see the impact of holes of different shapes and sizes which have been cut into wooden panels. The shape and placement of a hole affects its use. They have high play value near role play areas where the children can post items or talk through the holes.

Idea 13.5 Volume and capacity within your outdoor space

- When creating digging areas and sandpits in your play area, consider the size of these structures and their capacity. Generally, the bigger these play areas, the better.

- Think about the range of materials *in situ* in nature. The advantage of habitats such as beaches and woodlands is that there are a wide variety of natural materials for exploring volume and capacity as well as liberal quantities. Streams and other flows or bodies of water (including puddles) may also be available, especially on rainy days. Could you bring these elements into your outdoor space?

- If you do not have access to an outdoor tap, invest in some five litre and ten litre containers with taps so the children can access water. Water butts are another alternative that can be filled up with tap water or rainwater for the children to use.

Idea 13.6 Position and movement

Position and movement experiences within your outdoor space can be enhanced in different ways to aid children's understanding of perspective and scale.

- Create features that the children can move behind and spaces to crawl under, into or through. Think about the existence of nooks and crannies and create temporary ones through the provision of boxes or lattice screening if none exist.

- Provide small world play areas where the children can create features, position objects and move them about on a miniature scale.

- Ensure there is sufficient space for the children to set up obstacle courses and negotiate areas by themselves using wheeled toys, trolleys and programmable toys.

- As part of your participative approach to planning, create a map of your outdoor space which is easy for adults and children to refer to and use.

- Put up shelving in parts of your outdoor space. For example, in a mud kitchen there may be a cupboard for storing key items, hooks for hanging up spoons and so on.

Idea 13.7 Surfaces, stonework and tiling patterns and shapes

Paving stones and tiles are often arranged in geometric patterns. These can be used to:

- Inspire artwork.

- Investigate the properties of shapes.

- Illustrate the properties of shapes which tessellate.

- Explore and learn about symmetry.

They can also be used as flexible grids for graph work, position and movement activities and strategy games.

To involve children in the process of redesigning an outside space:

- Organise a visit with a group of children to a builders' merchant or landscaping business so the range of options can be explored. Consider the shape, size, colour and type of stone or material which can be used.

- Start collecting images of interesting designs. Search online for photos of geometric patterns from different cultures to provide ideas and inspiration. Ask parents and children to take photos of any interesting designs when visiting different places.

- Use to scale cardboard cut-outs to see what a feature might look like in a specific space. Sometimes an idea that looks good somewhere else just looks wrong in your space. This can help you and your children to decide on the precise layout.

Make available small loose stones that enable the concept of pattern to be explored. The children can experiment with building walls to discover which patterns of bricks are most stable. A small stone wall to which children can add or remove stones can be a much-loved addition to an outdoor space.

Idea 13.8 Paths

Paths invite play. They can be walked along or jumped over in different ways. The edges may offer an alternative route of travelling if clearly marked. Paths can be formal or informal. Shortcuts also have widespread appeal. Creating paths and trails is a natural activity in childhood which helps us to find our way and explore the lie of the land.

Networks of paths are forms of topological transformation (outlined in Chapter 9). Explore designs that allow the children to work out distances, routes, coverage of all the networks and how to get from one part of the play space to another. This also helps children to understand the flow of moving objects such as people and cars. Circular routes create lots of games potential and ongoing discussions about going round in different directions. Circuits also provide opportunities for trails, hunts and station activities.

Idea 13.9 Seating

Portable seats which children can move about can be used to develop the concept of pattern and the conservation of number when the layouts are changed in different ways.

Stumps have additional value. They can be cut from different tree species and polished to enable the concentric rings to be examined and counted. The children can compare the rings and variations between stumps.

Idea 13.10 Number hunt

Challenge the children to find and record all the numbers in your outdoor space. Consider the purpose and placement of these. Numbers can also be added by:

- Numbering resources such as gardening tools so that you and the children know how many of each tool there are. Systems are usually in place to ensure that tools are counted when handed out and returned.

- Having numbered places to put or hang objects.

- Numbering all the wheeled toys and creating parking spaces to match.

- Painting numbers on steps – start at zero and the first step up is number one.

- Keeping the labels on household junk materials that refer to volumes and amounts.

- Adding simple number scales to translucent water containers (e.g. marking one litre, two litre, and three litre lines on large containers).

Idea 13.11 Shadow numbers and shapes

Make number tiles from cardboard and put them in places where the sunlight can shine on them or through them to create number shadows. This is particularly pretty if coloured vinyl or Perspex numbers are used. You can place these on a transparent tarp or net above the ground. Very young children will enjoy watching the shadows move throughout the day. Older children may choose to chalk or outline the shadows or simply have fun jumping from number to number. A number mobile can create a similar effect.

Idea 13.12 Sundials and clocks

- A sundial can be placed where children can observe the movement of the shadow on a sunny day.

- Human sundials enable the children to cast their own shadow to tell the time.[4] They are very visual and involve physical interaction to work, but they do take up more space. There may be one in a nearby public park or garden.

- Hang clocks in windows so they can be read from outside. Draw attention to the hands on the clock at key times of the day.

---

4 For more information on sunclocks see: http://www.sunclocks.com.

Idea 13.13 Adopt a tree

Plant at least one tree so the children can photograph and observe seasonal changes throughout the year. The opportunity for every child to plant and care for a tree is worthwhile, especially if this can continue throughout the child's primary school years.

Idea 13.14 Zen gardens

A Zen garden can be a multifunctional place where patterns are prominent. They have plenty of natural features and surfaces that will provide year-round interest in all weather and seasons. The children may enjoy:

■ Creating line patterns with different objects.

■ Examining the detail in objects and patterns in nature.

■ Having time just to quietly be outside – a place to contemplate rather than run around.

An online image search will produce a multitude of Zen gardens which can be used to brainstorm the design and development of a space.[5] The children will need to think about:

■ The colours and materials used to create the ground and how these help reflection and thought.

■ Whether some features should be permanent, such as rocks, trees or shrubs, and what these symbolise.

■ The storage of tools for raking and making line patterns. Think about what tools are needed to create different line patterns.

■ Additional temporary objects which could be brought into the space to aid pattern making.

If you have a small outdoor space, then a miniature Zen garden can be created from cheap metre square raised beds. If you need to tidy up daily, then create a portable Zen garden in a beautiful box which can be put out daily in a quiet and calm corner.

---

5 Some useful starting points are mentioned in this blog post: J. Robertson, Zen gardens – a reflection, *Creative Star Learning* (9 January 2013). Available at: http://creativestarlearning.co.uk/developing-school-grounds-outdoor-spaces/zen-gardens-a-reflection/.

Idea 13.15 Mirrors

Looking at themselves in a mirror helps children begin to understand the concept of reflection. Put acrylic mirrors at different heights and in different positions outside. For example:

- Underneath a bench so the children have to crawl beneath it and look up.

- Behind a bush or inside a den to create the feeling of more space.

- Under a light log which the children have to lift up and look under.

- In a bucket of water which the children have to look into.

- As part of a pond or pool in a miniature world play area.

- Hang mirrors in natural areas such as amongst trees and shrubs. It can be surprisingly hard to see them.

- Convex mirrors can be situated on corners for looking around – just like a real spy!

Note: Some birds are confused by mirrors and can fly into them. Promptly remove any mirrors that cause distress to wildlife or reflect the sun's rays in ways that could be hazardous.

Mathematical gardening

Gardening is a valuable activity in any early years outdoor space. It seems a natural follow on from considering the design and layout of a space to include specific reference to a few of the mathematical possibilities associated with planning a garden, and preparing, growing and harvesting plants. It also serves to demonstrate the wide variety of maths skills involved.

Idea 13.16 · A perpetual, pictorial calendar

Create an annual calendar and use pictures or photos to help the children understand what needs to happen in each month. The Royal Horticultural Society provides lots of advice for schools and nurseries about gardening.[6] There are also many local organisations and horticultural professionals who can advise.

Idea 13.17 · Weekly rota of duties

Set up a child-friendly rota of duties such as watering, weeding, pruning and planting, so that children can observe when and how often each job needs to be done. Conversations can include:

- Estimating how long it will take to weed a raised bed.
- Finding out how much water a watering can holds.
- Discussing which weeds like growing the most in the garden. How do you know?

Idea 13.18 · What plants grow where?

A visit to a botanic garden or garden centre will demonstrate how plants can be classified. Look at the range of collections: herbs, trees, alpines, perennials and so on. Find out if a gardener can meet your group and answer questions from the children. Encourage them to take photos as a reminder.

After the visit, talk with the children about displaying and presenting their findings. Purchase some plants or put a call out for donations of plants to begin your own plant collection. Local seed exchange organisations may be able to assist. If you have a small space, grow small varieties in pots, raised beds or one metre plots.

---

6 See: https://schoolgardening.rhs.org.uk/home.

Idea 13.19 | The shape of raised beds and containers

If you are planting in raised beds and containers, then consider:

- Specific sizes to demonstrate scale.

- Using the same capacity but different widths, lengths and heights to demonstrate conservation of volume.

- Plots which follow golden ratio proportions. Discuss with the children whether these are more aesthetically pleasing than other rectangles.

- The layout that will most suit the needs of the children. Bear in mind the amount of space between the raised beds – there will need to be sufficient working space to enable the children to work safely with tools.

- Orientation. Some plants will need full sun and others partial shade, depending on the type of plants being grown. Use compass bearings to determine the aspect of your space.

- Traditional flowerbed or herb gardens. Some are based upon knot designs or laid out in wheels.

Idea 13.20 | Organising the gardening shed

Draw the children's attention to the maths involved as you collectively decide what goes where. This is about creating discrete sets where objects are sorted and classified according to their properties. For example:

- Create silhouettes for tools so everyone knows where each tool belongs.

- Spades may be hung between pairs of pegs to illustrate one-to-two correspondence.

- Seeds should be stored out of reach in labelled packets.

- Flowerpots can be stacked up.

Idea 13.21 Growing your own money

- Honesty (*Lunaria biennis*) has many names including 'money plant' and 'money-in-both-pockets' as the seeds appear on both sides of the silvery-white seed head. Some people keep a seed in their purse or pocket in the hope that it will bring financial good fortune. It may be regarded as 'fairy money' by the children.

- Creeping Jenny (*Lysimachia nummularia*) is also known as 'herb twopence' and 'moneywort' because of the shape of its leaves. The plant is low growing and quick spreading so can provide useful groundcover.

- Thrift (*Armeria maritima*) is a coastal plant that can be grown on rockeries and stone walls. It is believed that you will never be poor as long as thrift grows in your garden. If you can find an old threepenny bit coin from the 1930s or 1940s, thrift is featured on the reverse side.

Idea 13.22 Little and large

- Plant fast-growing climbers such as runner beans, hops and sweet peas along with sunflowers which can be easily measured. Discuss why plants grow to different sizes and which are taller and smaller than the children.

- Plant small, slow growing plants such as alpines.

- Use different sized pots or boots for planting seeds.

- Create miniature gardens, including terrariums or ones grown in sinks or tubs.

Idea 13.23 Heavy and light

- At harvest time, weigh the quantity of fruit and vegetables grown. Record and compare the yield year on year.

- Encourage the children to lay out the produce in order of size.

- Discuss and estimate which feel the heaviest and lightest. Does the mass of a fruit or vegetable match its size?

- Decide how to weigh the produce and what equipment may be needed.

Idea 13.24 Planting patterns

It is hard to garden without paying attention to patterns in various guises.

- Consider planting seeds such as lettuce in lines for easy identification and harvesting.

- Cut vegetables and fruit in different ways so the range of seed patterns can be observed. Have magnifying glasses available to look at the fine detail and patterns found.

- Planting out plants in clumps of odd numbers is often more aesthetically pleasing than doing so in even numbers. Plant up two beds side by side and compare the difference. How does this relate to rows of plants and planting schemes in public places? Take the children on a walk to find out.

■ Plant bulbs such as snowdrops, daffodils and tulips. Investigate whether they double in quantity year-on-year. Children can count the number of daffodils that are growing in each clump and then work out the total number of daffodils in the garden.

Idea 13.25 Harvesting vegetables and fruit

■ When harvesting vegetables and fruit, encourage children to find out how to cut some of the produce into halves. They may need assistance here. Then have fun mixing them up and putting the halves back together. This can lead to all sorts of conversations about perfect matches and symmetry.

■ Set up a market stall beside the garden so the children can sell the produce to parents, staff and friends. The children will need to consider:

○ How to lay out the vegetables in an attractive way.

○ How much water they think will be needed to wash the vegetables. What systems should be put in place to do this?

○ How they will weigh the produce.

○ How much to charge.

■ Use the produce for snacks. Get the children to take photographs and create pictorial recipes of their favourites.

Conclusion

To see a World in a Grain of Sand,
And a Heaven in a Wild Flower,
Hold Infinity in the palm of your hand,
And Eternity in an hour.

William Blake, 'Auguries of Innocence'

Through writing this book, I have engaged in many conversations with parents, outdoor educators, early years practitioners and maths specialists. It seems that the contribution of mathematicians to exploring the potential of any outdoor environment in the context of child development has yet to be fully realised. I hope that this book helps to raise this matter and also validates the role of the outdoors as a core place to learn – a source of intellectual inspiration for all children who can grow up excited by the abstract nature of our world as well as its other delights.

Messy Maths complements and extends the hundreds of blog posts which are on my Creative STAR website: www.creativestarlearning.co.uk. The 'I'm a teacher, get me OUTSIDE here!' blog began back in 2008. It's my way of sharing my enthusiasm for learning outdoors with the world. Please stop by, say hello and enjoy browsing many more ideas for learning outside in all weathers, all year round.

May your time spent outside and your interactions with children be steeped in the joy and wonder of maths.

Bibliography

Boaler, J. (2016). *Mathematical Mindsets: Unleashing Students' Potential Through Creative Math, Inspiring Messages and Innovative Teaching* (San Francisco, CA: Jossey-Bass).

Bryce-Clegg, A. (2015). *50 Fantastic Ideas for Mark Making* (London: Featherstone Education).

Corr, K. (2014). Outdoor play party – bottle babies, *Learning for Life* (31 January). Available at: http://nosuchthingasbadweather.blogspot.co.uk/2014/01/outdoor-play-party-bottle-babies.html.

Dunn, C. (2013). Racing to understand place value in EYFS, *Mr Shrek* (9 May). Available at: http://mr-shrek.blogspot.co.uk/2013/05/racing-to-understand-place-value-in-eyfs.html?spref=tw&m=1.

Eckersley, S. (2011). Handwriting, *Occupational Therapy for Children* (22 February). Available at: http://occupationaltherapyforchildren.over-blog.com/article-handwriting-67838149.html.

Haylock, D. and Cockburn, A. (2013). *Understanding Mathematics for Young Children: A Guide for Teachers of Children 3–8* (4th edn) (London: SAGE Publications).

Joyce, R. (2012). *Outdoor Learning: Past and Present* (Maidenhead: Open University Press).

Montague-Smith, A. and Price, A. (2012). *Mathematics in Early Years Education* (3rd edn) (Abingdon: Routledge).

O'Neill, D. K., Pearce, M. J. and Pick, J. L. (2004). Predictive relations between aspects of preschool children's narratives and performance on the Peabody Individualized Achievement Test – Revised: evidence of a relation between early narrative and later mathematical ability. *First Language*, 24, 149–183.

Patet, P. (2015). Empowering mathematical minds through play. *Community Playthings* (8 September). Available at: http://www.communityplaythings.co.uk/learning-library/articles/empowering-mathematical-minds.

Rhydderch-Evans, Z. (1993). *Mathematics in the School Grounds* (Exmouth: Southgate Publishers).

Robertson, J. (2011). More masking tape, *Creative Star Learning* (16 March). Available at: http://creativestarlearning.co.uk/early-years-outdoors/more-masking-tape/.

Robertson, J. (2011). Measuring sticks, *Creative Star Learning* (20 October). Available at: http://creativestarlearning.co.uk/maths-outdoors/measuring-sticks/.

Robertson, J. (2013). Zen gardens – a reflection, *Creative Star Learning* (9 January). Available at: http://creativestarlearning.co.uk/developing-school-grounds-outdoor-spaces/zen-gardens-a-reflection/.

Robertson, J. (2013). Daisy footprints – maths outdoors, *Creative Star Learning* (10 July). Available at: http://creativestarlearning.co.uk/early-years-outdoors/daisy-footprints/.

Robertson, J. (2013). Play in the dark – 10 ideas, *Creative Star Learning* (3 November). Available at: http://creativestarlearning.co.uk/early-years-outdoors/play-in-the-dark-10-ideas/.

Robertson, J. (2014). Rainbow maths sticks, *Creative Star Learning* (8 April). Available at: http://creativestarlearning.co.uk/maths-outdoors/rainbow-maths-sticks/.

Robertson, J. (2014). The clootie tree, *Creative Star Learning* (19 April). Available at: http://creativestarlearning.co.uk/early-years-outdoors/the-clootie-tree/.

Robertson, J. (2014). White line pebble maths, *Creative Star Learning* (12 July). Available at: http://creativestarlearning.co.uk/art-music-outdoors/white-line-pebble-maths/.

Robertson, J. (2015). DIY clipboard flower press, *Creative Star Learning* (14 May). Available at: http://creativestarlearning.co.uk/early-years-outdoors/diy-clipboard-flower-press/.

Robertson, J. (2016). Introducing Sammy the 1-metre rope snake, *Creative Star Learning* (12 January). Available at: http://creativestarlearning.co.uk/early-years-outdoors/the-magic-of-1-metre-rope/.

Soto-Johnson, H. (2016). Learning mathematics through embodied activities. *American Mathematical Society* (8 February). Available at: http://blogs.ams.org/matheducation/2016/02/08/learning-mathematics-through-embodied-activities/#sthash.LeIk8Lne.dpbs.

White, J. (2015). *Every Child a Mover: A Practical Guide to Providing Children with the Physical Opportunities They Need* (London: Early Education).

Worthington, M. and Carruthers, E. (2003). Becoming bi-numerate: a study of teachers' practices concerning children's early 'written' mathematics. Paper presented at the European Early Childhood Education Research Association (EECERA) conference, University of Strathclyde, 4–7 September. Available at: http://childrens-mathematics.net/paper_teachers-practices.pdf.

Ideas listing

Chapter 4 – Number Functions and Fractions 69

Chapter 5 – Money 85

Chapter 6 – Measurement 93

Chapter 7 – Time 119

Chapter 10 – Position, Direction and Movement 175

Chapter 11 – Data Handling 185

Chapter 12 – Routines 201

Chapter 13 – The Mathematical Garden 213

Index